THE MOON HAS ITS SECRETS

By

BARBARA MAKEDA BLAKE-HANNAH

Jamaica Media Productions Ltd.

P.O. Bo 727, Kingston 6, Jamaica

jamediapro@hotmail.com

CHAPTERS

CHAPTER ONE

AFRICA – 1684

The smell!

It was indescribable!!

Disgusting!!

Awful!!

The air was a stinking mass of the worst smell of nastiness ever gathered together in one place and time.

Kofia had never before smelt the stink of body waste of anyone except herself. In her village, each hut had a sheltered pit a distance away where they buried 'night soil' each morning.

Ever since she could walk, Kofia had become accustomed to the daily disposal of her own waste. It was a private ritual for each member of her village, who traditionally lowered their eyes respectfully when passing someone engaged in this activity.

This smell was the smell was of two hundred bodies that had nowhere else to evacuate their daily filth but right where they stood and had been standing for the past day, two days, four, five days, a week ... how long some had been there, no one knew. In this crush of human bodies, there was nowhere to sit, stoop or be private. Penned in like animals, they acted as the primal animals humans had been since creation. They pissed and shit where they stood, and tried unsuccessfully to dig with their toes some of the too-packed earth to cover their shame.

The filth oozed between Kofia's toes. After the first day when she was pushed into the cell and hemmed into the middle of the crush of people, she had managed to squeeze her child's body, little by little, through the mass of huge, sweaty, slippery male and female bodies to one wall of the airless, dark prison in which they were all crammed. Now she stood with her back against the wall. Here was the only spot where her heels, at least, were free of the stinking ooze.

Beside her was a woman whose smell was altogether different, though no less disgusting. At 14 years, Kofia was too young to recognize the smell of menstrual blood, but it would not be long before she too experienced the discomfort and distress the woman beside her was clearly feeling.

And the shame. Like the other women imprisoned in the holding pen, the shame of being exposed naked in front of strangers who were also all naked, was the cause of great mental distress. From this most shameful aspect of their imprisonment originated the wails of sorrow and bitterness, joining the moans of hunger and of pain from wounds and beatings, that filled the sound spaces around them all.

It was Hell, that place of utter darkness reserved for those who did not obey the sacred teachings of goodness and right action. It was a place where lived the demons with faces like the tribal masks in the ritual dances and ceremonies of her village and tribe, frightening, ugly masks with big red eyes, huge teeth, horns of feathers and bones, shrieking screams and rattling noisy shakers made of mysterious things. That must be where she was. In that place she had been terrified to hear about when her mother explained why she should be good and obedient and wise.

That place she hoped she would never experience.

That place she knew she did not deserve to be, not for all the days she spent too much time looking at flying butterflies instead of watching the cattle as closely as possible, not for the time she tripped and spilt a whole pail of water when the well was almost dried up in a long dry season, not for the time she punched her brother when he was teasing her, or the time she made a face at her mother's back after she had been scolded.

No, she reasoned with herself. She had long ago apologized and been forgiven, and those incidents were remembered by no one but herself. She did not deserve to be here.

Sometimes, above the din of sorrowing humanity rose the voice of a priest of one tribe or other in a language she could not understand, but speaking with word-sounds she understood that encouraged bravery and the pride in their upbringing and heritage, rather than sorrowful acceptance of their condition.

But otherwise, it was an unbelievable hell on earth in the airless, inhuman spaces where captured Africans awaited shipment to and enslavement in the Americas. None knew the horrors that awaited them in that new hell. All knew only that this was the most frightening, horrifying, terrifying, dehumanizing experience of their lives.

*   *   *   *

Leaning her head back on the mud wall, Kofia was able for the first time since her capture, to move her mind from the immediate condition in which she was struggling to survive and think back to her life and the moments that led to this time and place.

Five days ago, the morning air was as cool as the water of the nearby spring at which she filled the gourd slung across her chest beside the string of her bow and goatskin pouch of arrows. She was glad her breasts had not yet begun to swell on her chest, as they were starting to do on girls of her age in the village; nothing to get in the way of her important hunting tools. As she stepped softly towards the trees through the low grass around the village, Kofia's small feet crushed the leaves of a wild mint plant and the smell gave a perfect aroma to the quiet peace of the day's beginnings.

Even as a girl, Kofia was trained up from her earliest years in the arts of agriculture and war: her daily exercise was shooting and throwing javelins; and her mother adorned her with emblems after the manner of the tribe's greatest warriors. In this way Kofia grew up till she was fourteen, on the day when an end was put to her happiness.

That morning, when all the adults were gone out to their works as usual, Kofia decided to try her skills of hunting out in the woods by herself, leaving her youngest brother to mind the house.

Today she would show them. Today she would prove she was as good as any boy child. Today she would make a kill and bring food back to the village, like the boys did who laughed at her helpless envy as they sauntered out each day, happy and carefree, to roam the forest and low savannahs spearing small animals and strengthening their bravery. Kofia's mouth was set firm as she moved through the familiar country, her spear stamping the ground softly in front of each step.

Why was the pleasure of hunting denied to girls? What was it about girls that decreed that they should never take delight in the hunt, in the victory of capture, with the pride of provider? I am as strong as they are, taller than most of them. I throw my spear and shoot my bow and arrows more accurately than any of them.

Stretching her neck proudly and thrusting her head towards the treetops, Kofia inhaled the sweet smells of the jungle, heard the rustle of leaves, the clicking calls of insects, the flap of birds' wings. She greeted with a smile the low branches that brushed against her body and playfully snatched at the loincloth hanging from a braided leather belt around her hips – her only covering.

Here she was at home, at peace.

This was heaven.

I will show them today, Kofia assured herself. I know the paths they use to reach the best game. I have followed them secretly many days, with their noise and rough play and waste of time, giving the game lots of time to run away. It will be better on my own. I will stalk the game quietly, aim perfectly and kill without pity. I will be brave. I will be strong. I will be victorious.

As she walked, Kofia reflected on her life this far. At fourteen years she would soon be married to one of the village elders, who would take her from her mother's home to live in his compound at the center of the village. She was still a child, a girl changing into a woman. She would be a prize for any husband. Her legs were long and the muscles strong. Her arms were firm and her shoulders wide from practice with the spear. Her entire body shone with health. Still, there seemed to be no hurry to have her married. As her breasts had still not yet budded and her boyish frame not yet begun to fill out into the desirable curves necessary to interest a man, the process was somewhat delayed.

The delay also had a lot to do with the fact that Kofia had always been a 'difficult' child, a girl given to a certain firmness and independent spirit that was unheard of for a female, but which was excused and rationalized as the indwelling of the ancestral spirit of a powerful, respected tribal priestess. When Kofia would stamp her foot and refuse to perform a domestic chore, instead of punishing her, the other women would simply raise their eyebrows, spread their lips tight around their teeth and mutter "Tata Kofia" under their breath, as much to identify the ancestor after whom she was named, as well as to pacify the resurrected spirit they felt they recognized in Kofia.

Kofia was as respectful as expected to her mother, and to her grandmother and grandfather with whom they went to live after Kofia's father – their son – was killed in a lion hunt when his daughter was five years old. Kofia's grandparents often told her stories about her father, how brave he was, how famous he was far and wide for the many lions he had killed before finally being killed by the biggest, baddest lion that had ever terrorized their village. Kofia's mother would sometimes weep silent tears when she overheard these stories, showing poignantly that she missed her husband deeply and the love they had both shared, underlining even more fully to Kofia what a good man her father had been.

Kofia's father was, of course, a much older man – a seasoned warrior. Kofia's mother was married to him when she was aged 14 herself. A widow with one daughter at age 28, village tradition doomed Kofia's mother to permanent domicile with her husband's family as, with no man to provide for them, the duty rested with her dead husband's family.

What stupid rule was this, Kofia reasoned to herself, that denied her mother the physical help of her children and doomed her to a life as a beggar? What would happen to her mother when her father's parents died? Kofia knew it was her duty to marry and provide a home for her mother to live with her there.

But somehow this was not what she wanted for her life, an endless domestic drudgery. An image of her father loomed like an invisible presence in Kofia's daydreams and even in her night dreams. She felt the brave blood and the brave heart of her father in her, knew that she was his daughter and knew that a part of her would always want to live that brave blood and brave heart in ways for which there were no opportunities for women.

Kofia raised her water gourd to her lips and drank. She had been walking for half an hour from the village and it would be good to rest now, to be fresh for the last mile to the small hill overlooking the animals' water hole, from which she would select, stalk and kill her prey. She thought about what kind of animal she would kill from among the many gathered at the waterhole. A gazelle perhaps, or an eland. Good food, tasty meat. Not a crocodile, lurking in the dark water to snatch a small doe strayed too far from its mother. Not an elephant, for sure. Too big.

She smiled. Kofia loved watching the elephants from her secret hideout, moving in slow, heavy, precise steps as they splashed water over their giant bodies and cooled down. She loved to see the love mother elephants shared with their infants, so tender and human-like.

Sometimes Kofia would stare entranced, as a cheetah or a lion stalked the herd of gazelle, chased one down and killed it, dragging it off to the far trees where others waited to help devour it. The blood did not frighten Kofia, nor the kill. It was life in death, and life itself was merely a prelude to death. Even in death, her father was still alive, an ancestor reverenced by the stories told by grandparents, though mother, to child.

There was no death if life had been lived nobly, a life worthy of praise and remembrance. That was the lesson Kofia had learned from her father's life and death.

Suddenly Kofia was startled to hear the sound of cries coming from the direction of her village.

The children! My brother! Oh NO!!! The Oye-Eboe!"

The Oye-Eboe! The capturers! She had heard the talk from the elders that the red haired men who traded captured prisoners and spared villages the trouble of executing them, had turned to capturing villagers when there were no prisoners to trade. This was a dangerous new threat to centuries of the African tradition and the village was aware that its people were liable to be attacked.

Still clutching her weapons, Kofia raced back the way she had come. Branches slapped at her face and body as she ran through the bushes that grew under the tall trees. She should not have left the children alone. She should not have ventured out on this bold adventure. Tears stung her cheeks as she ran. She could hear her brother cry out her name.

"Kofia! Kofia! Help!"

But then his voice stopped calling and the sounds instead were of big men shouting in a language she did not understand. Kofia ran towards a point west of the village, towards a track she knew the body snatchers would travel to escape. As she ran, she shouted:

"Leave them alone! Leave the children!"

She reached the village out of breath to find people running around wildly, women trying to grab children, to escape, to hide. Kofia saw her brother running towards her and she grabbed him, then turned to see where they could run. Several men jumped over the village walls, and in a moment seized Kofia and her brother. Without giving them time to cry out or make resistance, they stopped their mouths with pieces of bark, tied their hands, and then marched them off into the nearest trees. It was as sudden as that. With whips and brutality, they pushed everyone into a line, linked their ankles together with metal chains and forced them to walk forward into the jungle. They continued walking, their cries joining the cries and moans and pleas for mercy, for release, from the villagers, the slavers shouting at them and whipping them with lashes and sticks when they stumbled or protested.

Helping the red-faced men were several brown-skinned men in long garments and cloth tied on their heads to protect from the sun. They led the party of captured villagers as far as they could till night came on, when they reached a small house where the slavers halted for refreshment and to spend the night. Kofia and her brother were then unbound, but were unable to take any food and, being quite overpowered by fatigue and sorrow, their only relief was sleep which came as a gift from a kind god.

The next morning the party of slavers and enslaved left the house and continued traveling all the day. Once they came to a road and saw some people at a distance. Kofia began cry out for help, but her cries only made her captors hit her, then tie a cloth in her mouth again to stop her speaking.

The only comfort for Kofia and her brother was in being in each other's arms all that night and bathing each other with their tears. But alas! Kofia was soon deprived of even that small comfort, as she and her brother were separated early the next morning while they lay clasped in each other's arms. It was in vain that they begged not to be parted. Her brother was torn from her tight embrace and immediately carried away to join another group of enslaved men and boys, while Kofia was left in a state of total sorrow. She cried and grieved continually and for several days did not eat anything but what was forced into her mouth.

The walk to this place where she now was has taken 8 days of pain and sorrow. The bitter memory of her parting from her beloved brother and protector, washed Kofia's face with tears again. She wished she was dead. She might as well be dead, to be in this place.

Kofia was awakened by movement and noise around her. The mass of humanity that pressed against each other in the pitch-black space was waking to the angry shouts of the red-faced devils that screamed through the small peepholes in the thick iron door of the underground cell.

"We are leaving!" Kofi heard a voice say in her language. "They are setting us free! Come! Hurry!"

The deep fear, sorrow and anger that clouded every mind, stirred expectantly at this good news. It was all a big mistake! Soon, they all believed, someone would apologise to them for the barbarity, cruelty and injustice of their capture and imprisonment, they would walk outside into the free, fresh air and be set free to return home to the faces and embrace of the people they loved. Kofia would see her brother again. She smiled at the expected joy.

Those still chained together caused chaos as others tried to press through the narrow door, and it took several minutes for Kofia to find herself in a stream of humanity moving forward. Step by step, inch by inch they pressed towards the dim light that shone outside. Freedom lay outside and every black body urged itself to grasp that freedom that had been denied them since their capture.

The sight that greeted Kofia's eyes as she reached the exit door was like nothing she had ever seen in her life. She seemed to be standing at the edge of the earth. In front of her the earth ended, and all that could be seen in the distance was a vast body of dark green water. What was left of the land was covered with a moving, stumbling mass of black humanity, moaning and groaning, shrieking with fright, pain and horror. This was no freedom, no apology, no. It was a greater and more hellish prison than they had ever seen.

Before Kofia the surging, heaving mass of dark water stretched endlessly in front of the strip of land. Kofi had never seen so much water in her life, not even the broad rivers that coursed through her native lands. This water was angry, swelling in heaving waves, belching and spitting forth mountainous gulps of foamy, dark water. What was this awful place? It was indeed the place where bad souls went, worse than the place she had just left.

Bodies floated by the shore of people who had died of fright, injuries, or given up life rather than face the hell before them. Women moaned, big men howled. Around Kofia a chorus of sorrow and despair rose like a satanic choir in the morning air. Vultures swooped in frightening surges towards the shore, pecking at the flesh of dead bodies.

Strange-faced men shouted at them, lashing with whips and sticks to make them move forward along a pier jutting out over the edge of the water. At the end of the pier was a large canoe with wide sides, into which the strange-faced men were pushing them to enter. Falling and jumping with shrieks of fear and pain, Africans were filling up the boat, while another waited nearby to take its place as it was rowed out by other strange-faced men, some of them Africans dressed like them.

Far out on the dark water floated two strange wooden houses with large white cloths flapping from tall tree trunks planted in the center. Between the shoreline and the houses on the water, small boats filled with naked black human bodies were being rowed towards the floating houses by muscled arms under the shouted directions of the strange-faced men, who also carried the shooting sticks that all had learned could pierce a body and kill or leave painful wounds.

Kofia's curiosity about the large water and its strange sea-borne houses was soon to be filled, as the press of humanity around her soon brought her to the edge of the sea and sooner still, falling into the bottom of one of the canoes. Kofia had paddled her brother's dugout canoe downriver many days, steering through the sweet flowing water while her brother trailed a fishing line. A flood of memories of beautiful moments brought a rush of tears to Kofia's eyes. The pain of losing her brother pierced deep.

But then the memories strengthened her and she brushed off the tears, determined not to seem weak. "I am a warrior princess," she reminded herself, and held her head higher as she sat, crushed into the boat's cramped humanity. Her mind took her back to the firesides where she sat beside her mother at night, listening to the tales of the men recounting their victories. Her mother would croon in a low voice, singing the mantras of strength.

"I am a warrior princess. I will not bend. I will remain strong, even to death."

Kofia closed her eyes and braced herself against the swelling surge of the canoe on the water, closing her ears from the shouts of the red-faced men and the moans of the others beside her.

"I am a warrior princess. I will not bend. I will remain strong, even to death."

Then the canoe came alongside the house on the water, and Kofia found herself being hauled by the arms up the side of a ladder on which she barely placed her feet, before being flung like a sack of rice onto the deck.

*   *   *   *

CHAPTER TWO

THE ISLAND

1494

Columbus left Cuba on July 22, turning southeast towards Jamaica. He spent the next month exploring the western and southern coasts of the island. He was fascinated by the beauty of the countryside and he observed the many excellent harbours and the fruitful nature of the land. There were Taino villages all along the coastline and from each of these the people followed the caravel in their canoes. They brought offerings of their fruit and other foodstuffs for the newcomers and Columbus said that his crew preferred their foodstuffs to any other that they had tasted in other islands.

Sailing south-easterly around the western tip of the island, Columbus could see from his preliminary inspection that this island was heavily populated. He was fascinated by the Taino. Spain, from which he had sailed, was so different. Metals were in common use; pottery and glass works had reached a high level of development. Silk, satin, rich jewels, precious stones, other luxuries from the Far East reached his country via long arduous overland routes and it was in order to find new sea routes that he had set out. However, here in this island was a race of people who enjoyed a simple, primitive life, dependent on nature, even though wars with neighbouring tribes were sometimes inevitable.

So began the encounter, on a friendly basis, the best fruits of the Indians being offered in exchange for European novelties. Columbus set up the Spanish standard and declared that he had taken the island in the name of Spain, calling the island Santiago.

The encounter with the Taino in Jamaica was to become of great significance to Columbus and the Spanish conquistadors, for in successive years Jamaica proved to be the market basket for support of Spanish expeditions into Central America. The particular feature which made this food so important was the long shelf life of the cassava cakes they made which enabled the Spaniards to ship it to new colonies located hundreds of miles away from Jamaica.

The Spaniards forced the Taino in the earliest form of slavery, placing themselves in full control over the native *people, their assets and their lands. Immediately the negative impact on Taino life was evident, as the industrial approach to farming was not in keeping with native tradition. Their alternative action was to move themselves to the lower mountain slopes and establish themselves in the thick bush in the John Crow and Blue Mountains in the east– the first Maroons. Those Taino in the west of the island retreated to the Carpenter Mountains, while those along the Negril and Montego Bay coastline simply found it more convenient to sail their canoes to Cuba.*

The Spaniards were moved to import slave labour and in 1513 Esquivel was granted permission to import three Africans as his household servants. This practice of acquiring black servants was then fashionable in Europe and had been popular in sections of North Africa for a long time, where rich merchants purchased youths from Moorish traders who had acquired them from the lands south of the Sahara desert. These first slaves came from the Bakongo or upper Angolan people. Many were educated Africans, knowledgeable in the sciences, in astronomy and the crafts, for the Bakongo were well-known ironsmiths and fluent in several languages, especially Arabic – the language of culture and science. Spain had conquered Granada, a Moorish settlement on the Iberian Peninsula, in

1492, and the captives of this battle were the source of the first slaves. These first Africans bringing their culture with them were able to adapt to their new circumstances. Intermixing with the native Tainos, they would one day comprise the largest ethnic part of the runaway slave population – the Maroon people.[1]

PLANTATION JAMAICA

The most considerable and valuable of the British West India Islands, Jamaica lies between the 75th and the 79th degrees of west longitude from London, and between 17 and 18 north latitude. It is of an oval figure, 150 miles long from east to west, and sixty miles broad in the middle, containing 4,080,000 acres. An elevated ridge, called the Blue Mountains, runs lengthwise from east to west, whence numerous rivers take their rise on both sides. The year is divided into two seasons, wet and dry. The months of July, August, and September are called the hurricane months. The best houses are generally built low, on account of the hurricanes and earthquakes. However pleasant the sun may rise, in a moment the scene may be changed; a violent storm will suddenly arise, attended with thunder and lightning; the rain falls

---

[1]   The Maroon Story: The Authentic and Original History of the Maroons of Jamaica – 1490-1880. Bev Carey, Agouti Press, 1997

*in torrents, and the seas and rivers rise with terrible
destruction.*

*The mountains that intersect this island seem
composed of rocks, thrown up by frequent earthquakes or
volcanoes. These rocks, though having little soil, are
adorned with a great variety of beautiful trees, growing
from the fissures, which are nourished by frequent rains,
and flourish in perpetual spring. From these mountains
flew a vast number of small rivers of pure water, which
sometimes fall in cataracts, from stupendous heights;
these, with the brilliant verdure of the trees, form a most
delightful landscape. Ridges of smaller mountains are on
each side of this great chain; on these, coffee grows in
great abundance; the valleys or plains between these
ridges, are level beyond what is usually found in similar
situations.*

*The highest land in the island is Blue Mountain
Peak, 7150 feet above the sea. The most extensive plain is
thirty miles long and five broad. Black River, in the
Parish of St. Elizabeth, is the only one navigable;
flatboats bring down produce from plantations about
thirty miles up the river. Along the coast, and on the
plains, the weather is very hot; but in the mountains the
air is pure and wholesome; the longest days in summer*

are about thirteen hours, and the shortest in winter about eleven.

In the plains are found several salt fountains, and in the mountains, not far from Spanish Town, is a hot bath of great medicinal virtues; this gives relief in the complaint called the dry-bowels malady, which, excepting the bilious and yellow fevers, is one of the most terrible distempers of Jamaica.

The general produce of this island is sugar, rum, molasses, ginger, cotton, indigo, pimento, cocoa, coffees, several kinds of woods, and medicinal drugs. Fruits are in great plenty, as oranges, lemons, shaddoks, citrons, pomegranates, pineapples, melons, pompions, guavas, and many others. Here are trees whose wood, when dry, is incorruptible; here is found the wild cinnamon tree, the mahogany, the cabbage, the palm, yielding an oil much esteemed for food and medicine. Here, too, is the soap tree, whose berries are useful in washing.

The plantain is produced in Jamaica in abundance, and is one the most agreeable and nutritious vegetables in the world: it grows about four feet in height, and the fruit grows in clusters, which is filled with a luscious sweet pulp. The Banana is very similar to the plantain, but not

so sweet. *The whole island is divided into three counties,*
Middlesex, Surrey, and Cornwall, and these into six
towns, twenty parishes, and twenty-seven villages.

This island was originally part of the Spanish
Empire in America, but it was taken by the English in
1656. Cromwell had fitted out a squadron under Penn and
Venables, to reduce the Spanish Island of Hispaniola; but
there this squadron was unsuccessful, and the
commanders, of their own accord, to atone for this
misfortune, made a descent on Jamaica, and having
arrived at St. Jago, soon compelled the whole island to
surrender.

Ever since, it has been subject to the English; and
the government, next to that of Ireland, is the richest in
the disposal of the crown. [2]

---

[2]"Prince: Narrative," *Microsoft® Encarta® Africana 2000.* © 1999 Microsoft Corporation. All rights reserved.

CHAPTER THREE

THE ARRIVAL – 1685

It was here that the slave ship docked to disembark its gruesome cargo – an island as full of natural beauty as it was with the horror and brutality on which its brilliant sun shone.

Kofia, like the other survivors in the ship's stinking hold, hurried up the planks to the deck, eager to taste fresh air again. The sight that greeted her eyes took her breath away. The ship lay at anchor in a turquoise sea whose colours faded into pale creamy white as it lapped at a sandy beach. The land was covered with huge trees, some bearing bright blossoms, and the sky was a clear blue with few puffy clouds.

It was not Africa, but it was almost as beautiful.

But the land, sea and sky were not able to hold her attention for long, as before her on the dock the process of herding chained Africans to a holding cell was being

organised by a team of burly, sweaty red-faced men, some
of whom had been their merciless captors on board, and
several Africans who were distinguished from the chained,
naked ones by the fact that they wore shirts and pants of
coarse cloth.

Those who were sick fell on legs made weak by
confinement, some were blinded by the bright sunlight,
some retched from stomach ailments, women wept. As the
Africans stumbled onto the pier, they were herded towards
a long table at which sat several red-faced men who
examined them and noted their age, sex and condition in a
large ledger. Each African was then chained at the ankle to
a longer chain and, when there were 20 persons chained to
each length, the line of humans was led off towards a large
wooden building close to the wharf filled with many red-
faced men drinking, shouting and examining the
merchandise as it passed by.

Outside that building was a large open barracks into
which each line of Africans was released to sit or stand as
and where they wished. Naked men and women shouted to
each other, hoping to find an answer in their native tongue.
Some cursed the devils that had delivered them to this
pagan place, some searched for lost relatives or friends,
some shouted across the pen, asking where they were and

what was happening. Some sent up prayers to their God, Muslims knelt down as best they could, uttering cries to Allah. Women wept, especially those who had been separated from children or husbands in Africa, and those who were clearly pregnant.

Kofia recognised her language being spoken by a woman, crying out loud and weeping. She moved quietly through the crowd until she stood behind the woman. Pinching her firmly on the buttocks, she hissed into her ear:

"Where is your pride, stupid woman?" The woman clapped her hand over her mouth and turned around, displaying a face streaked with tears and dirt.

"Behave like a princess, not a child," said Kofi, angrily. "Never forget the lessons of our elders."

Still sobbing, the woman looked into Kofi's eyes. "Are you not afraid too, little girl?"

"Yes mother, but I refuse to show it before these strangers," Kofia replied. "Don't worry. Let us stay together until we learn what is to be our fate. We will keep each other strong."

With an arm around her shoulders, Kofia led the woman to a part of the pen where they could sit. The woman put her head in Kofia's lap and fell asleep. Beside them, a man and woman with their fingers interlaced nodded a greeting and approval of Kofia's actions.

Soon the noises of self-pity, sorrow and fear quieted down, as people grew tired and rested. Some talked to others who spoke the same language, or whom they had come to know while chained in the ship's holds. A large, steaming urn of thick cornmeal was brought into the barracks and there was a rush and crush of bodies trying to get food or to wait for a bowl to become empty so they could use it.

The woman still slept, so Kofia did not move. She knew that if she should wait until the crush had lessened, the food might be shared out, but she sighed and decided to do without, if necessary.

Night had fallen, and through the spaces between the wooden planks of the barracks walls, slivers of light announced that there was a full moon outside. Kofia sat, thinking back on all that had happened to her since she was so shockingly taken from her home and country. She closed her eyes to hold back tears, as she remembered the trees and blue skies and happy life behind her. It was hard to think about what she had lost, and worse about what was ahead. How would she survive, she asked herself.

Then she remembered something her mother had taught her one Moon Night, as they sat outside their home under the silver light. When she was ten years old, Kofia's mother had begun these Moon Night lessons that she told Kofia had been taught her by her own mother. Kofia remembered her grandmother as a quiet, serious woman who held her ancient frame with the regal grace of a queen.

"The moon is a woman," said Kofia's mother, "and so it has power for the woman who knows how to use its powers. A woman can speak to the Moon and get its help to do anything she wants. This is one of the most important secrets of the tribal priestesses that I will give you, my daughter."

"I am a tribal priestess?" Kofia asked.

"Yes," her mother replied. "The line is handed down through me to you and you must hand it down to your daughter too. We have special duties to perform for the village and the tribe. You must learn them all so that you can be a good leader."

"What should I say when I speak to the Moon?" Kofia asked.

"Say these words first, then tell the Moon for the help you want." Leaning to Kofia's ear, her mother spoke four words. Kofia repeated them.

"Not so loud!" her mother had hissed. "These are secret words that only the priestess must speak, because the power can be used for harm by those who secure it."

Now, sitting in the darkened barracks lit only by the glow of the moon outside, Kofia repeated the words softly, as she remembered them. She repeated them again. Then deciding to test the promised powers, she spoke the word "Food."

Someone bent down before her and handed her a bowl of cornmeal. It was the woman who had been holding hands with the man. She pushed it towards Kofia, speaking words in another language that clearly meant "Here. Eat."

Kofia bowed in thanks as she accepted the bowl, dipping her fingers into the now-cold food and eating gratefully. The smell woke the woman sleeping in her lap, and together they ate from the bowl, wiping the sides clean with their fingers.

The words worked! Kofia smiled. Now she had a weapon. The Moon Night Secret. Her mother would be proud. She wiped the tears that sprang as she remembered her mother, and her family. But when she remembered her father, she forced the tears back.

"I am Strong. I am a Warrior Princess. I shall LIVE"

*   *   *   *

The next morning their captors herded everyone out of the barracks and into a big yard, at one end of which a platform had been erected. There was a well in the yard and some Africans wearing clothes were hauling up buckets of water and throwing it over the naked Africans with gestures that indicated they should clean themselves. Shivering and embarrassed, the new slaves washed themselves as best they could, and waited.

Kofia saw a crowd was gathering on the other side of the platform, but what a strange crowd it was! The men were all red-skinned like the ship's crew, but by their fine clothes and the way they strutted about, laughing and talking with each other, these were important people. Some smoked long pipes, some drank a brew from metal goblets, others a hot brown liquid poured into white cups.

Kofia could not understand the language they shouted to each other, but she understood the contemptuous glances they gave as they looked over to the penned Africans. Separated by gender, one by one the Africans were led onto the platform, while a red-faced man standing on the platform pointed at them and shouted some words to the gathering. One man in the crowd would shout back to him, then another, and another. Then the first man would hit his table with a piece of wood and the African would be led away to another section of the pen where the red-faced man awaited him or her.

Women hung their heads and tried to cover their nakedness, as the man on the platform lifted up their breasts, pried open their mouths and slapped their buttocks. Men tried to protest when their privates were lifted, squeezed and examined. But there was a man who seemed to enjoy using his long, coiled whip to open a bloody slice of flesh on the back of any African who protested. He had many opportunities to display his expertise with the whip.

Kofia shuffled along the line of women and children. Some wept silently, tears rolling down their cheeks. Children wailed until they were silenced by an adult or by fear of the mercilessly administered whip.

Then it was time for Kofia to step up on the platform. "I shall hold my head as high as if I was wearing my weapons and my war girdle," she told herself. She pointed her face and eyes above the crowd and, since she could not understand the words being shouted at and about her, she mentally recited the warrior words she chanted before going out to hunt. "Make me brave. Make me strong. Make me victorious....make me brave. Make me strong. Make me victorious."

Yes, she could be brave. She could be strong. That would be the victory.

In less than a minute Kofia was grabbed by the arms and led off the platform to a large wooden cart harnessed to two donkeys. On the floor of the cart, five men and another woman sat on dried leaves of a large grass that she would soon come to recognise as sugar cane. Finding a spot beside the woman, Kofia sat down. She looked around at the other faces, but none would look into her eyes. So she sat and waited.

Soon another man joined them, then a woman. To Kofia's joy, it was the woman she had spoken to in the barracks, who had slept in her lap. "God is good," the woman greeted her, a smile breaking across her tears. "At least we have each other." Hearing the women speak, one of the men greeted them in their own language.

"God is truly good," he said, folding his palms together in the traditional greeting. "We have come from far together, but Allah has seen fit to make us family in this hell. Let us remember the traditions of our culture and help each other as best we can."

"Stop talking!" The voice in their language came from one of the Africans wearing clothes, who stood beside the cart. "You will live longer if you keep your mouths shut." His voice was loud and angry, but his face seemed to be offering good advice, rather than condemnation. Kofia realized that many of the clothed Africans came from her native country.

"What place is this," she whispered to the man.

"The Native Arawak Taino peoples who used to live here called it the Land of Wood and Water, XAYAMACA," he said.

"Now be quiet!"

One of the red-faced men walked up to the cart and spoke to the African. The African pushed some logs between slats at the rear of the cart and secured them with chains that imprisoned Kofia and the other seven inside. Then he mounted the front of the cart and whipped the donkeys, which lurched forward and started the cart rolling along the dirt road.

The African who had spoken to her picked up a piece of cloth from a corner of the cart and handed it to Kofia. "Cover your shame," he said. Kofi took the dirty cloth and tore it in half, handing a piece to the other woman. Then she knelt in the cane trash and wrapped the cloth around her waist like she did when she went hunting. The other woman followed her example, and both felt more at ease in the presence of the men. Kofi knew it was a great disgrace for strangers to see her nakedness, and she was grateful to the man who had helped her.

Looking through the slats, Kofia could see the cart was following a horse-drawn box on wheels. Once when they stopped to rest the animals, Kofi saw a door open in the box and a red-faced man step out to speak to the African.

The cart followed the buggy for several hours along a road made by the double tracks of hundreds of wooden wheels over many years. As night fell, the air grew colder, the Africans in the cart pulled other pieces of cloth around them. Kofi had used her cloth to cover her nakedness, so she endured the cold like the warrior she knew herself to be.

"I will be brave. I will be strong. I will be victorious." She repeated the words softly to herself, and forgot about the cold.

It was dark night when they reached the edges of wide fields flattened out of the thick forest of trees. The African on the cart began to beat a piece of metal loudly and the noise was answered by sounds of other metal being beaten in the distance. Soon Kofi could hear shouting, as people roused themselves. Then the light of lamps became visible in a large building set in the center of the fields, as the buggy and cart entered the gates of the Plantation.

People came running out to greet the buggy and help the red-faced man alight and remove several parcels. The red-faced man got out of the buggy and walked up to a large house, on the verandah of which stood three African women dressed in long skirts, aprons and head-ties. As he stepped into the house, the women bowed, then followed him inside.

Then the cart rumbled around the side of the house some distance to a low, long hut, and stopped there. The newly purchased Africans were herded out of the cart in which they had been traveling, separated into male and female groups, then led to the slave barracks.

In the female barracks Ama Katurna stood watching the newcomers arrive, a massive Black woman whose serious face and shouted commands showed she was to be obeyed. Kofia was pleased to hear the woman speak in her language.

"Salaam Alaikum" she greeted the large woman.

Ama Katurna turned a scornful face to Kofia and spoke: "Here we speak the Massa's language. You can start learning it now."

A bundle of cloth was tossed to each woman. Kofia picked up hers and found it was a large sack that had once contained flour and which now had holes cut in the bottom and sides to make a smock. Pulling it over her head, she found a space on the dirt floor between other female bodies and, drawing her feet up like a baby, she lay down and finally slept.

Kofia's new life had begun.

* * * *

CHAPTER FOUR

THE GREATHOUSE

On the first morning Kofia was told to join the women assigned to the plantation Great House and learn housemaid duties. The large house was built of limestone blocks, two sturdy stories with a wide stone staircase leading up to the top floor residence of the Massa and his family. The ground floor, standing on stone arches, housed the kitchen and work areas of the many house servants, whose jobs ranged from preparing and cooking food, keeping the house clean, and serving Master and Missis Parkins and their two children, aged 5 and 3 years.

The large open fire in the kitchen was always burning, cooking three meals a day for the Parkins, as well as dinner for the three bookeepers, also Englishmen, who serviced the plantation and lived in smaller houses set at a distance from the Great House, each with a smaller retinue of servants.

The Great House stood at the top of a rise that overlooked the entire estate, hundreds of acres of flat land carved out of the forest jungle and neatly laid out in green rows and rows of sugar cane, occasionally interrupted by small hills covered in shady trees. Far away at the bottom of the estate, the stone funnel of the sugar mill rose above the landscape, its huge continually turning water wheel powered by the stream that ran through the Parkins estate and its fire constantly being fed by the strongest of the enslaved men.

Beside the mill house stood other buildings that housed the barns, tool sheds and storage bins; beside those were the cattle pens with cows, for milk and beef donkeys and mules for plowing and reaping, and a chicken house. Not far from the mill were the rows of low barracks where the labour force of Africans slept and lived, the coconut palm thatched roofs covering walls made of sticks daubed with mud to make a thick and sturdy clay. Behind the barracks small garden plots were visible where the Africans raised some crops.

Cleaning the windows of the lookout atop the Great House Kofia could see the sea shimmering in the far distance, a turquoise jewel that beckoned enticingly. It could have been beautiful, yet it reminded Kofia of the horrors of the journey that had brought her and so many from Africa to this island.

Tears filled Kofia's eyes, but a sharp clap to the side of her head whipped her around, to see a plump older African woman looking at her fiercely.

"Get hold of yourself!" she barked at Kofia. "Do you want a lashing? You can make it easy for yourself, or hard. Weeping makes it hard."

And as she turned to walk back to her duties, "I am Ama Katurna. Pick up that broom and follow me!"

$$*\qquad*\qquad*\qquad*$$

Kofia soon learned the daily routine of hard work that were her duties. Her youth and her lack of understanding of the native dialect the slaves had created from many tribal languages so they could speak to each other, meant she needed to be trained. Where better than behind the wide aprons of Ama Katurna, who had earned the trust and respect of the white Mistress to be allowed to be in charge of the women serving inside the Great House itself. Katurna said that Kofia looked like they both were tribal relatives and she taught her not just how to clean and wash, but the many serious lessons she needed to learn for her survival.

"Lesson One: Never look a Massa in the eyes. He will think you think you are his equal. You are not his equal."

"I see." Kofia nodded. "Massa is the Chief, like in our village. We may not look him in the eye either."

"And also the Massa wife. And the Children too. All the pink-skin people."

"The children are Chiefs too?"

"Yes. Even the youngest White person in this place is always your superior. You must do whatever they want. That way you will avoid the lash."

"That will not be an easy lesson to remember. A child is the least in our village. But I will try."

"Lesson Two: You may not sing or show any form of happiness."

"There is nothing to sing about in this place." Kofia frowned. "That is an easy lesson to learn."

"Be careful of this one! There will be a day when a sad song will come into your mind and heart, and your mouth will open. Shut it quickly, or the lash will sing with you."

Kofia bowed her head, and bit her lip to stop the tears that welled. "Oh yes, you are right. The songs of sadness can spring as unbidden as the songs of joy."

"Lesson Three: Very important lesson. Forget about the country we were brought from. Forget that you were ever there."

"I can NOT do that!" Kofia almost screamed. "I can NEVER forget Africa! One day I will leave this place and return home!"

"You cannot return. WE cannot return."

"WHY?" Kofia stamped her foot. "Is everyone too afraid to try? I will show these coward men!"

Ama Katurna folded her arms across her big bosom and stamped her foot also.

"Listen to me girl! Don't you remember the big ship you came here in? Do you remember how many days and nights we floated on the ocean, before we finally set foot on land again in this place? How do you plan to return? How will you get a boat? Even if you could get a boat, could you row a boat by yourself that many days and nights over the waters?

She slapped Kofia once again on the side of her head.

"I know that didn't hurt, because your head is hard... won't take in learning!!!"

*   *   *   *

These and other lessons filled the endless days of Kofia's new life.

The GreatHouse was the engine that kept the estate running. Massa Parkins would rise early to receive the report from the chief gang boss that work in the fields had started. Another report came from the mill, where the machines were being repaired and oiled in preparation for the grinding of canes and boiling of juice. Then he would sit with the overseers discussing the business of the estate.

The planting and reaping of sugar cane, its conversion into juice, sugar, molasses and rum, had a rhythm that had been set to deliver a volume of product in the quickest and cheapest way. The rhythm was kept beating by strokes of the lash that administered pain to those who fell short of the necessary work. Field work was brutal and only the infant and sick were spared its brutality.

Kofia listened to a gray-haired man talk one night in the shadows of a tree where some tried to escape the heat of the crowded barracks.

One day we was working ... cutting Penguin grass to plant at Springfield – old Sally was chained to a young girl name Mary; it was heavy rain time; driver was pushing the people on to run fast – was flogging them on, the young girl was trying to get on and was hauling and dragging the chain that was on him and Sally neck, as Sally don't able to keep up; at last, the old woman fall down, right in a place where a stream of water was running through the negro-house street, and she don't able to get up again, then the driver stand over her with the cat, and flog her, but she not able to get up with the chain on, so he take off the chain and make the young girl tie it round her body, and go along with the rest; then he stand over the old woman and flog her with the cat till he make her get up, and keep on flogging at her till she get to the cook's fireside; the old creature stand there trembling and wet up – for two or three hours she not able to move away, she look quite stupid; all the other people in the workhouse quite pity this poor old woman, and it would any body heart grieve to see her. The under-driver tell the head-driver one day, that if him keep on eat her so, some of these days she will dead under it, and then he will get into trouble; every day I was in the workhouse, except to Sunday, I see them beat this old woman.[3]

Later, lying on the rough cloth that covered a pile of coconut branches in her space on the barracks floor, Kofia visualized the scene the man described and realized how carefully she would have to live in this place, to avoid such pain and humiliation. She would stay close to Ama Katura and follow her example and instructions.

The softest couches in the world are not to be found in the mansion of the slave. The slave bed is a plank twelve inches wide and ten feet long, the pillow a stick of wood. The bedding is a coarse blanket, and not a rag or shred beside. Moss might be used, were it not that it directly breeds a swarm of fleas.

The cabin is constructed of logs, without floor or window. The latter is altogether unnecessary, the crevices between the logs admitting sufficient light. In stormy weather the rain drives through them, rendering it comfortless and extremely disagreeable. The rude door

[3] NARRATIVE OF EVENTS, By James Williams, an Apprenticed Labourer in Jamaica; Publisher: J Rider, London

hangs on great wooden hinges and at one end is constructed an awkward fire-place.

An hour before daylight the horn is blown. Then the slaves arouse, prepare their breakfast, fill a gourd with water, in another deposit their dinner of cold bacon and corn cake, and hurry to the field again. It is an offence invariably followed by a flogging, to be found at the quarters after daybreak.

Then the fears and labors of another day begin; and until its close there is no such thing as rest. The slave fears she will be caught lagging through the day; she fears To approach the mill-house with her load of sugarcane; at night she fears, when she lies down, that she will oversleep in the morning. Such is a true, faithful, unexaggerated picture and description of the slave's daily life.1

*   *   *   *

The Great House was the largest building Kofia had ever seen. Perched on a hill overlooking the entire estate, it stood on stone foundations rising high enough to house the kitchen, pantry for storing foods like ground provisions, salt, salt meats and fish, the laundry room for ironing and folding clean clothes (for the washing was done in the estate stream), a small room with beds for the butler and night servants, and a large empty space to house the estate buggy.

A stone staircase from the ground swept upward from the ground to the first floor of wide, shady verandahs surrounding the mahogany floors of the large hallway, the living and dining rooms and the Master's study in which he conducted business. Up a wide staircase on the second floor were bedrooms for Massa and Missis Parkins, one for their two children and the nurse that slept with them, a drawing room for the Missis, and the Massa's library in which he maintained the records of the plantation's business. All rooms opened onto the verandah, overlooking the fields of sugar cane sweeping in the distance towards the Trelawny coastline.

The Great House was a showpiece of ornate mahogany furniture, upholstered velvet, needlework cushions, damask drapes, crystal chandeliers, fine china, silver tableware and gold-framed oil paintings, for the Parkins were determined to create a replica of English country life in the middle of the Jamaican tropical jungle. The house slaves who worked hard to maintain this lifestyle and take care of the needs of the Massa and family, were a little higher on the plantation heirarchy than the field slaves – though so much closer to the seat of authority that they were always the first to receive physical punishment for minor infractions, even such as singing.

There in the Great House Kofia learned how to polish mahogany floors, to build a fire, fetch and carry water for the mistresses' daily bath, how to serve food at table and, the worst job of all in Kofia's opinion, making soap to wash the large bundles of cloth worn, used and discarded to be laundered at the river each week. There Kofia learned that the work of a house slave was no less hard than a field slave, the difference being the work was mostly indoors and out of the sun. Mostly, except washing clothes.

Washing not only required both strength and caution because it involved building a large fire out in the wash yard, heating water on it in large iron tubs, then using soap made from lye and tallow that burned her fingers, bringing water and clothes to a boil and then removing them without scalding herself. In the beginning she wasn't always able to avoid being scalded, but after enduring the pain of badly scalded feet and hands one sleepless night, she made sure it never happened again. Ama Katurna gave her a broad leaf of aloe to wrap on her burns and she soothed the pain all night with its slimy healing power.

Sometimes Kofia was sent to the river to pound some of the dirtier items clean on big, smooth river stones. That was harder work and the river was some distance away, especially carrying a large basket of clothes, but Kofia preferred this task as it gave her a moment to enjoy the beauty of the river, the river plants, the small fishes playing in the rock pools and the brilliant birds darting through the trees.

These were the only moments when the child in Kofia, interrupted so brutally, emerged for a moment of free spirited joy. This place of pain and suffering could be as beautiful as Africa, with different masters in charge of everyone's life and work. She tried to think of what life could be like with such changes, but there seemed no way out of the present condition, in which those who owned her and kept her captive held power with such brutality and immorality.

*   *   *   *

After 3 years as a slave at the Parkins estate, by the age of 17 Kofia was no longer a girl, but a woman in all but years. Broiled by the sun each day, her skin shone like polished ebony, contrasting the strong white teeth and bright eyes that illuminated her face. Her youthful body had filled out with fat, thanks to the slabs of pig meat and cow offal that were fed to the Africans; despite their disgust at eating the forbidden animal all eventually realized that food was better than starvation. Kofia's flat chest had grown into breasts the size of small gourds and her hips grew wider, as her stomach swelled round to join the fleshy mounds of her buttocks that provided a thankfully soft cushion in rare moments of rest.

She was now mother to one child. Her son's father was Big Sam, the plantation stud, whom the Massa had purchased as breeding stock for the young African girls he owned. Kofia knew what was in store for her the night Ama Katurna came to take her to Big Sam, for it was the Ama herself who had told her what to expect and how to deal with it. It was no less or more than the actions that accompanied the sounds Kofia heard around her at night, when men would creep into the corners of the women's quarters to visit their lovers. She did as she had been told, ignoring the pain and surprise of Big Sam's entry into her body.

But she had not enjoyed it. And she had been brought to repeat it many more times, to her disgust, until she was glad to find herself pregnant and relieved of her unwelcome duties. When her son was stillborn, she was not sad when she was told it had died.

What followed was worse. Ama Katurna took her one night to the Great House stable where, in a pile of dried grass, Massa Parkins did to her what Big Sam had done, with even more force, cruelty and disgusting behaviour than Big Sam. It was traditional, said Ama Katurna, when a slave baby was stillborn that the Massa would 'fertilize' the slave's womb himself. Kofia had no idea that the girl child of the pregnancy that resulted would be born with skin the colour of honey. The sight of the child's pale skin and un-African features, the result of what she considered a experience with a devil, made her hate the infant. She was glad when the baby was handed over to a wet nurse, to join the other slave babies being brought up without parental attachment in the hut where they would grow and learn to live their lives as slaves.

Kofia was sad to have brought another human being into the life she was being forced to live. The pain, brutality, inhumanity, torture, blood and murder she had seen in her years on the plantation, were a maddening force of anger within her mind and heart. She hardened her mind and heart to the thought of her daughter and the life that lay ahead for her. She felt no attachment to a child born of such horrifying circumstances.

What was it, she asked herself, that gave anyone the power or right to be so evil to other human beings? Was it really true that the colour of her skin was not beautiful – as she had been taught all her life, but a mark of evil that gave those without that mark the right to inflict such pain, brutality, inhumanity, torture, blood and murder on people whose skin were the colour of hers? Was it really true that this teaching of the God of the pink-skinned people was right, and the teaching of our god ALLAH, may his name be blessed, was wrong?

Kofia considered. But Allah is never wrong. This is what is evil. This is a test of Allah to see if we are strong enough to overcome this work of evil. A test, indeed. For these pale-skinned, pale-eyed, pale-haired creatures were not human! They were a special breed of devils that had flown down to earth like evil scavenger birds. Only devils could be so evil! They could kill a man without touching him with the fire that comes out of a stick and pierces a body.

Where did they get their magic from? Only the devil that looked just like these monsters – pale-skinned like lepers, fierce, angry, with no knowledge of love or of the Divine Creator before whom all must bow.

CHAPTER FIVE

THE COROMANTE

"Oh I wish I was a man!" Kofia expressed her thoughts like a strong breath.

Two men sitting close by her waiting to have their clothes washed, nudged each other and laughed.

"Why is that, my sister? You like hard work?" one asked with a smile.

Kofia did not even realize she had spoken out loud. She jumped and covered her mouth with her hand.

"I'm sorry, I ...." she thought quickly, then smiled and said:

'No, maybe because I don't like hard work. Maybe if I was a man I would offer to help the woman nearest to me carry her heavy laundry load, and then maybe if I was a man ....."

Kofia smiled and the man answered her smile.

"Well now, you don't have to be a man when you have a man right beside you, so give me the basket and I will be happy to help you." He smiled with anticipation. "Have a seat and rest a moment."

Should I? Kofia wondered. Why not?

She smiled back and sat on the ground.

I need to stop thinking so deep, she thought to herself. A few moments of normal conversation would be a blessing in this place of hell.

She looked at the man who sat down beside her. He was tall and slim with long, strong legs and arms. His skin was the colour of the earth after the rain, a deep brown with a healthy shine and his teeth were white and even as he smiled. His head was shaved clean and polished like a shiny globe.

As he took the basket of clothes and set it beside him, she saw his hands were large with long fingers that had the parchment look of good hard work. She liked his face. The high cheekbones marked him as a Coromante, member of the warrior tribe that were said to be fearless, and feared.

"What work do you do?" Kofia asked. "I haven't seen you before. Are you new here?"

"No, I am not new. I have been here three years," he smiled his reply. "I am a craftsman. I built the Massa's house."

Kofia was surprised to meet a craftsman, and impressed. Craftsmen were slaves with special skills as ironmongers, tailors, artists who knew how to carve lumber into beautiful furniture, or to construct a house in the English way with mahogany staircases and cedar floors over cut-stone foundations. Slaves with these crafts got special treatment because of their special skills. No wonder he was down here lazing away the morning, like he was a massa.

"A craftsman!' Kofia smiled at him. "I never met one before. You must have a happy life, don't you?"

The smile left the man's face. He took Kofia's hands into his own and looked very seriously into her eyes.

"How can I be happy giving the best of my skills for free to people who kidnapped me and brought me here, far from my home, my family, my friends, my language, my history, my future children? How can I be happy? Tell me, my beautiful sister."

Kofia's heart raced. The man's words inspired the warrior spirit in her, hidden but never forgotten from the Moon Secrets she had learned from her mother as a young girl in Africa. It made her heart race to be held with the strong hands of this man, to look deep into his eyes and feel the strength of his spirit. This was a man she would be happy to lie with, to share his body, to bear his children. Kofia felt herself tremble as her body responded.

"I see you share the same hope as I, to be free to see my beloved home again." She removed her hands from his, before her trembling gave away her inner emotions.

'Is there anyone here who does not share that hope?" he was serious.

'Only fat Adassa, Mistresses' favourite. She thinks the Mistress is going to set her free and take her to live in England with her," she laughed. A smile crossed his serious face and Kofia was glad she had made him laugh.

"My name is Kofia. What is yours?"

'My name is Quamin. I am a Coromante Ashanti." There was pride in his voice.

"I am happy to meet you," Kofia spoke the truth. "I don't often meet men like you in this place."

"There are only a few of us who are Coromante here. The slave-masters like our skills, but they are afraid of us because we do not like being slaves. We are always trying to get away from this bondage and live free once again." Quamin shook his head.

"In our country we have slaves too, we take slaves to work for us, increase our population and serve in our army. But in our country slaves have rights. In our country, slaves can own property after he has served for a number of years, and if the slave will take the religion of our people and believe in Allah, the child of a slave is a free person. Owners do not murder their slaves unless the King gives permission. These white slave owners are cruel and wicked. I cannot remain under their rule. They have no rules!"

The conversation was getting interesting but dangerous. Kofia wanted to say a lot, but said nothing. The Coromantes were always ready for rebellion, running away and getting lashes. It would not be wise to let this stranger know how much she agreed with him. Kofia got up and started to pick up the basked of wet clothes.

"I have to take that laundry back to the Great House now. They will be wondering what is taking me so long."

The man stood and smiled. "Are you afraid of what I said? Don't you want to be free too?" He reached out a hand to hold her back. Kofia knew he could feel her trembling. She turned and raised her eyes to his.

"I am not afraid. I am warrior woman too." She threw her head back and lifted up her eyes to his.

He smiled. "That's what I thought."

No more words were necessary. The two started back on the path towards the house, with Quamin carrying the basket and following her. As they walked, he spoke.

"We must talk some more. I can come and visit you in the women's quarters. Do what you must to get the corner space."

Kofia knew what he meant.

"You are very bold to think I will ever meet you in the corner space! I don't know you!"

Kofia made her voice angry, but she knew she was only pretending. She wanted to meet this man again, she wanted to hear him speak again about freedom. But most of all, she wanted to be embraced by this man's hands and body, to melt into him and make him a part of her and to remain so always, locked in the fullness of a man and feel him as the perfect other half of her whole. Kofia felt perspiration on her upper lip and feelings in her body she did not understand, but welcomed.

She would have to barter with the elder Nana who supervised the women's lodge with a precious item stolen from the Great House -- a piece of satin ribbon or a table knife -- or do some extra cleaning duties, to get the right to take her bed-roll to the corner of the lodge where a man could slip under the hole at the bottom of the wall and have some small privacy to embrace the woman who waited for him there.

"Don't disappoint me." Quamin looked at her seriously as he handed her the laundry. Kofia bowed her head to hide her smile and took the basket from his hands.

"I plan to run away," he said softly and urgently. "Come with me. I need a woman to have my children."

Kofia was shocked and speechless. This was too much, too soon. She hurried into the laundry room, flustered.

"You' crazy, have Coro man following you around." Esmie turned from stirring the boiling pot of white clothes. "Coro-man is just trouble, you know that," she hissed disapprovingly.

"Me don't know him," Kofia would give nothing away to Esmie. "Him just help me with the basket."

But she knew she would wait for him one night soon, and many, many more after that.

Kofia took a sudden liking to laundry duties at the riverside, always hoping to see Quamin on her walk there or back. She sometimes walked another way to the river that passed the furniture shed where he built and repaired the Great House chairs and tables. Once he blew her a kiss from a sawdust-covered hand and she blushed, which gave Esmie who was also on laundry duty, still more reason to frown and sniff.

"You are Great House slave, him just a yard labourer," she spat at Kofia.

"You think you better than him?" Kofia smiled. "He have a trade, him can earn money; you and I are just house niggras, good for nothing."

"Me good for something Massa like," Esmie strutted her fat bottom in front of Kofia.

"You can keep THAT work, me no want it again," Kofia was angry.

"You never know when you get a call for that work again, Congo gyal, and you better not be angry when it come or after the beating Massa will give you that time, you will only good for field work or get sell." Esmie knew she spoke the truth.

Kofia did not care. Quamin was the first thing of goodness she had found in the hell of the plantation. She would not hold back from enjoying the small joy of knowing him, having someone who had the same thoughts, who was surviving without giving in, who still had the prideful way of an African man. His wide smile, his gentle voice and the unspoken words that passed between them, gave Kofia a reason for living each day and she looked forward to every chance meeting they had.

And early one morning, as she hurried to the river to rinse out a special blanket that had been soiled, she caught sight of Quamin bathing in the river. He was standing in the knee-high water, one arm raised above his head as he lathered his body with a handful of leaves. Their eyes met for a brief moment, till modesty made her lower her gaze, but not before she had seen his body glistening black in the river water, a tall, slim body, muscles on thick arms, wide chest and back, a strong flat stomach descending to a place of interest, the memory of which continued to flood Kofia's mind with thoughts she had never before had.

Oh, how she longed to be pressed close to that body, Kofia thought all through the day. Each time she remembered that brief moment,she smiled and shook her head. Such thoughts were impossible dreams, just for personal pleasure in the hard plantation life. But that was the first time she offered to wash some clothes for the woman who slept closest to the hole in the barracks wall, in exchange for a night's sleep there.

And so it began.

*   *   *   *

CHAPTER SIX

TWO WHIPS

Other eyes saw the growing interest between Kofia and Quamin. Brandon, Massa's buggy driver stood beside the carriage horse waiting at the side of the house for his next assignment. He was short, stocky and had a lumpy growth on his neck, but his job carrying Massa to important meetings of plantation owners, to slave markets in Falmouth and regular tours of the estate's many hundreds of acres, gave him access to special gifts of food, clothing and money that made him attractive to many of the plantation's women.

"Why walk when you can ride?" he bared broken teeth at Kofia, stroking the buggy whip, sliding one hand repeatedly along its plaited length to the horsehair ends, then flicking it with a slight crack.

Kofia looked at him fearfully. She knew how viciously Brandon swung his whip at any slave walking along the road, when he drove the carriage by himself. She had heard, too, that Brandon forced women who befriended him for what he could give, to feel the sting of the whip on their naked bodies whenever he felt like expressing his sadism sexually.

Kofia did not answer. One sideways glance and a polite nod of her head was all she dared.

Brandon laughed out loud as she passed. "Ha Ha Ha! "You 'fraid? Don't be afraid of Brandon. I will love you better than that Coro man."

Kofia rushed away as his voice like an animal's growl followed ears and her mind back to the laundry room.

A week later Brandon made a new approach. He had driven the Massa and his wife to Duncans a week before for a medical checkup of her third pregnancy, and the house maids were busy cleaning and getting the house ready for their return. Their gossip and chatter was the usual speculation on which pregnant or nursing mother was going to be given the job of wet nurse when the child was born.

The Mistress did not suckle her own children – that was not the custom, especially as she suffered from periodic bouts of malaria which not only laid her up in bed for days and sometimes weeks, but especially so that the babies might be nourished by healthier, stronger milk.

The job of wet-nurse could be a good one to have only in few circumstances, such as when one of Nana Odugo's twins died and she was glad of its replacement on her large and empty breast, even though the sight of black and white babies sucking together was often cause for surprise and even laughter.

But it was not good when a mother's baby was deprived of the nourishment it had brought into the world with it, for it. Those babies grew weak, small-boned and miserable and the mother pined for her child, while having to give loving, protective care to a stranger's child. It could be a terrible punishment, but some had taken the pain and used the opportunity to gain favours, such a lighter duties or even a promise that her own child would not be sold away from her – a promise rarely kept.

Kofia was doing her weekly duty of polishing the wide mahogany staircase that swept from the living room to the upstairs rooms of the GreatHouse. The polish smelt of cedar and eucalyptus and Kofia was on her knees pressing and sliding a pad of cloth along each step to shine and polish the wood, as she heard the women chat and laugh.

Suddenly, Kofia felt her skirt pushed roughly up over her buttocks, her pantaloons pulled down and the unmistakable feel of a solid muscle of flesh pushing into her private place. With a cry and a swift shift of her body, Kofia flung off her assailant, who fell down the stairs with a crash that exposed Brandon flat on his back, with the fly of his pants unlaced and a flap of brown flesh falling out of the opening.

There was silence, as the other maids stopped to watch the scene with horror. Brandon raised himself up, picked up his whip and glared at Kofia with the ugliest face she had ever seen.

There was a silence that seemed endless, as Brandon caught his breath. Then he spat on the floor and spoke.

"Think you are too good for Brandon, eh Congo girl? You don't want Brandon?

Brandon going to make you sorry, very sorry for this. Very sorry."

And looking Kofia straight in the eyes, he reached to a nearby table for a portait of Massa and his family framed under glass, and smashed it to the floor.

Kofia gasped! It was one of the most precious things in the house, a treasure of which the house maids were continually told 'Be careful!' as they dusted.

"Why did you break Massa's picture, Congo girl?" Brandon shouted.

"Me!" Kofia was shocked. "I didn't touch it. You broke it!"

Brandon turned around to the women who were frozen, watching, mouths open.

"You all saw what she did, didn't you?" he asked, "You saw this lazy Congo girl break the Missus picture. Now, who going to say different?"

His eyes moved from face to face to face, burning each pair of eyes with his expression of anger and hate that forced them to drop their eyes and turn their heads away, with neither answer nor denial.

Brandon turned to Kofia, his face now a triumphant sneer.

"Who do you think Massa will believe, when I drive him back today and tell him you broke Missis picture? And what do you think he will do to you for breaking their silly picture? Wait and see, Congo Girl. You will be sorry you refused Brandon."

Kofia turned to the other women. "But you all saw what he did! You saw! Say something!!!"

Kofia turned around to look at each woman. Not one met her eyes. They looked away and pretended to return to the work they had been doing. Kofia fell to the floor, and wept.

With a snap of his whip that made a sharp CRACK over Kofia's head, Brandon turned and swept out of the house and down the stairs. Shortly all that could be heard was the clip clop of horses' hoofs and the grinding of carriage wheels racing out of the plantation gates.

The friendly noises, the smiles and happy chatter that had been the mood while the Massa was away, had suddenly reverted to the fearful eyes, angry faces, the head-bent shuffle that was their normal behaviour. As they averted their minds from Kofia, they knew what was in store for her and they dared not seem to sympathize with her in case they also were made to share her fate.

Kofia lay sleepless that night in the women's lodge, her mind following every turn of the carriage wheels that Brandon was driving, bringing the Massa back to the

Plantation. She could almost hear the crack of his whip, and the drumbeat of the horses' hooves on the road, as she thought about the lashing she was soon to receive.

A lashing was not an unusual, or pleasant, event on Massa Everett's plantation. Kofia had witnessed more than enough examples of what she was soon to experience, what she had prayed never to experience. It was not the pain she knew she would receive, bad as she knew it would be. More than the pain, was the humiliation, the degradation of being stripped, bound to a tree and subjected to as many lashes as would satisfy Massa's desire for satisfaction or revenge for whatever action he felt had been worthy of that lashing. Worst of all, was knowing the injustice, the hatred, the total and complete WRONG for which she would be beaten.

As she lay on her bedcloth Kofia remembered her mother, it was now five years since she had last seen her mother, since she has last walked in the free air and sky of her home, Africa. Kofia shed two small tears, but the tears angered her and she rose up and walked through the line of sleeping women outside into the night.

Stupid girl, she admonished herself. What are you crying for? You are not a weakling. You are a warrior woman, born in the pure earth of Africa.

A new moon was shining a soft light and Kofia remembered the teachings her mother had given her on Moon Nights in Africa.

"You are a warrior woman. You have inherited the Moon Secrets from me, who inherited them from my mother. You must remember the Secrets and pass them on to your daughters when they are born. Remember always to be brave, always be strong," she had said, "and you will be victorious."

"I will be brave. I will be strong. I will be victorious." Kofia repeated the words softly.

"I will be brave. I will be strong. I will be victorious."

Kofia planted each foot strong on the ground, folded her arms over her chest and breathed a deep gulp of the cool night air. As she swallowed it, she felt a strength come into her, an unknown spirit that bound itself to her closely like her hunting spear had been. She felt a protective embrace cover her, like when her mother hugged her as a child.

"I WILL be brave. I WILL be strong. I WILL be victorious."

Kofia knew she was speaking the truth.

*   *   *   *

There would be no work on the plantation this morning, until the lashings were over. The slaves were summoned by a pounding of the gong and all 60 were now assembled in the yard in front of the Great House.

There were two other slaves to be lashed before it was Kofia's turn. A runaway, the man they called Johnny, but who said his name was Ben Ahmed and who had run away before, who said he was trying to reach the Maroons in the hills. Massa picked the biggest of his slave drivers, Manny, to administer the whipping, a big brute of a man whose whip kept the cane field workers hard at work.

He rode a donkey up and down the rows of cane, his huge body straddling the small animal from which he jumped from time to time to administer whippings as he wished. Whipping Johnny delighted him, and he smiled as he delivered each of 50 blows that Ben Ahmed took with his teeth gripped and his face and eyes forward, unflinching.

Next was Old Nelly, a gray-haired old woman, the only one on the plantation who knew the healing herbs and roots that kept them all well, kept evil away and, she promised – could help a man fly back home. Massa had found and seized her bag of roots (yes, there were also some dried bats, lizard skeletons and a small skull in it) and Massa had cursed her as an 'African witchwoman'. So Manny did not hold an ounce of his strength back as Old Nelly wailed and begged for mercy, called to her African gods in her language, cursed Massa, the beater, and all the slaves who stood watching helplessly in silence, until she finally sank into a silent heap on the ground, oblivious to the lashings that continued to rain on her beaten body.

Then it was Kofia's turn. She had been kept waiting, hands tied behind her back. Now she was untied and roughly dragged over to the tree around which her hands were made to embrace before being tied together at the wrists, as her dress was ripped apart to expose her back. She could see the Mistress standing beside her husband, looking at her with anger and contempt.

"Damn clumsy wretch!" Mistress spat at her. "Perhaps you did it on purpose to spite me! I hope they beat you good!!"

Manny raised his hand to bring down the first lash but as he did, Brandon stepped forward to the Missis standing beside her the Massa and bowed.

"Excuse me please Massa, if I can have a word... I know how much Mistress go miss that picture. Your servant Brandon would grateful to punish her meself, Mam, give her the lashing personally for you. It would be an honour for me Massa." He smiled and bowed again.

The Mistress looked to her husband, who frowned first, thought about it, then nodded his permission. Brandon's smile grew wider. He walked over to the whipping post and, rejecting Manny's lash, he uncoiled his buggy whip from the holder at his waist and flicked it. It whistled and then cracked loudly, some watching jumped at the sound, and even more at Brandon's laugh that followed it.

"*No!*" Kofia screamed. Or she thought she had screamed. But no sound had come from her mouth. Only her mind.   She turned her head and looked Brandon directly in the eyes.

"*I WILL be brave! I WILL be strong. I WILL be victorious!*"

Again she spoke with her mind.

"I will be BRAVE!"

The first lash landed searing pain like fire and acid from shoulder to hip.

"I will be STRONG!"

The second one landed on top of the first and the fire grew hotter. Kofia has never known such pain.

"I will be VICTORIOUS!"

Kofia was determined that Brandon would get no satisfaction from her pain. She clenched her teeth and gripped her hands into strong fists. She took deep breaths of air between each lash.

"I will be brave ...

I will be strong ...

I will be victorious...

I will be brave ...

I will be strong ...

I will be victorious..."

Brandon gave a yell of joy each time he flashed his whip through the air to land on Kofia's back. She could hear his grunt of joy as each lash landed.

"Oh Allah! How did I sin so much to deserve this?"

Kofia's mind talked to her deity. The pain was unbearable. She had thought she could bear it, but the sting of the lash was strong enough to sweep her body sideways with each stroke. Kofia bit her lip, closed her eyes, and drew breath and strength between each bitter slap of stinging leather strips on flesh.

At the 7th lash Kofia opened her eyes. Someone was calling her in her mind.

"Open your eyes Kofia!" the voice said

"Open your eyes! Look at me!"

Kofia's whole body was concentrating on making the pain bearable. Closing her eyes tight made it bearable. She could barely open them.

But she did.

And she was glad she did.

Standing in the crowd of slaves, but directly in her eyesight, was the Coromante. He stood with his feet apart and his arms folded across his chest. His forehead was a furrow shading his eyes, which were fixed on her and now locked into her eyes and mind and as if into her body itself.

"*I see you,*" Kofia said to his eyes.

"*I will stay with you to the end,*" his mind said to her mind.

"*I am strong ...* " she said.

"*I am brave ...*

I shall be victorious ...

I am strong ...

I am brave ..."

"*You will be strong, you will be brave, you will be victorious...*"

And he stood there, holding that position, looking straight into Kofia's eyes through every lash of the whip. It was strange how his eyes made Kofia's pain disappear; how suddenly the lashes had no feeling just a sound of whip and its connection with flesh.

No pain at all.

No pain ...

Kofia did not know when the lashing ended, how many strokes she bore. She did not remember when she was untied from the tree and carried back to the women's lodge, where another woman just as wise and knowledgeable as Old Nelly was waiting to spread soothing gel from several fat aloe vera leaves onto her bleeding, ripped skin, to give her some tea brewed from a bag as deep and as mysterious as Old Nelly's, and lay her to rest and recover a night and a day and another night and another day.

It was over.

Just some pain and then healing.

*   *   *   *

But it was not over.

She woke the second night to find the Coromante man sitting on the floor beside her in the dark of the healing hut.

"How...?"

Kofia struggled to speak, raising herself off her stomach to her elbows.

"Shhh." He pressed his fingers to his mouth.

"Don't speak, just listen. I come to tell you to be ready to leave here at any moment, day or night."

"Leave here? How? Go where?"

Kofia was puzzled. After 3 years, she knew that leaving the plantation was something everyone wanted, but she knew also that the attempt would result either in death or a terrible beating on recapture.

"Don't worry. Just be ready. I will come for you." He gently touched the crusts of scab covering the welts on her back. Kofia winced.

"Not healed yet. I will come when you are fully healed," he said. "Just be ready."

As silently as he had entered, he disappeared, leaving Kofia to wonder, and to hope.

*   *   *   *

CHAPTER SEVEN

THE ESCAPE

Life on the plantation returned to its labourious and wretched routine. Healed or not, Kofia was sent back to work – this time no longer in the Great House, but in the sugar cane fields, a life to which she was as yet unaccustomed.

The big slave Manny ruled over the rows of men, women and children digging, planting, weeding and cutting the sweet grass. The sun was hot, and while an old rag shielded her head from the unaccustomed and boiling sun, the heat of its rays penetrated through the thin cotton flour bag that served to cover her body, and inflamed the sore welts on her back.

Stooped down beside an older woman, Kofia copied her actions as best she could, making every effort to avoid the lash which Manny smilingly seemed ready to inflict on her for any mistake. It took a week for Kofia's back to harden, and her mind to grip firm on her reality. No self-pity for her. The key she held that kept her strong was the brief words the Coromante had whispered in her ears that dark night.

"Was it my imagination, brought on by the fever?", Kofia wondered. But no, to confirm her doubts she recalled the unforgettable memory of his eyes that had held her mind and soul like magnets as her body was being violated by Barry's lashes, and the mental strength from those eyes that had made her as strong as the iron of the spear tip she had carried on the day she was captured from her village.

'Patience," she told herself. "He will come."

*   *   *   *

It was several weeks later one moonless night, that Kofia felt her shoulder being shaken to wake her.

"Shhh..." A woman put a finger over her mouth. "Come! Bring your bedcloth and wear your sandals."

"Who are you?" Kofia was surprised.

"The Coromante sent me to bring you. We are leaving. Come."

Kofia did not question. She had seen the woman when she worked in the Great House, who would bring foodstuffs from the plantation garden to the kitchen. Kofia rolled up her few personal things in her bedcloth and followed the woman as she lifted up the corner of the hut for both women to creep out under. The woman walked swiftly to a clump of trees on the edge of the river that fed the estate waterwheel. As they reached, Kofia felt strong arms grab her and enfold her in them. It was the Coromante.

The woman embraced another man who stood in the shadows. It was 'Johnny' the runaway who said his name was Ben Ahmed, who had been whipped before Kofia.

"We are leaving this place of the Devil," said the Coromante. "Ben Ahmed knows the way to the lands where live the people who have freed themselves. He let himself be caught, so he could come back for me, for us."

Kofia well understood the warrior spirit that would make a man endure the pain of a lashing to rescue a fellow warrior. The religion of these two men united them in a moral code that was completely opposite to the people under whose imprisonment they had lived. Now she understood that this was going to be a serious attempt to runaway.

"Let us go then, before they find we are gone and set the dogs after us." Kofia was ready. She picked up her bundle in which she had placed a few useful things.

"Not just yet," said the Coromante. "We have one last thing to do before leaving. Follow me."

Turning, he headed through the bushes in a path that circled the slave barracks. By the edge of the men's huts, he stopped and placed a finger to his lips, then knelt down to creeping position, as they all did. Crawling silently towards one hut, he paused outside the palm leaves of its thatched wall, then with one swift motion slashed an opening through and, followed swiftly and silently by Ben Ahmed, jumped into the hut and onto the sleeping form of two bodies.

The bodies jumped up, one a man, one a woman. But before either could make a noise, a hand covered each mouth. The woman was flung on her back, with Ben Ahmed's hand on her mouth. The man was held in a kneeling position by the strong arms of the Coromante.

Kofia and the woman pushed the dried palm leaves aside as they also entered the hut, giving enough light to see. It was Brandon.

Swinging Brandon's head around to face Kofia, with only a whisper, the Coromante said to him: "Look at her. This was your mistake."

His mouth still covered with one strong hand, and feeling the cold of a machete under his throat, Brandon spread his arms in a plea for mercy, looking Kofia straight in her eyes. It was good to see her cruel torturer so close and so helpless. Kofia gathered up a large mouthful of saliva in her mouth and, aiming carefully, spat it straight into his eyes.

Then before Brandon could blink to clear his eyes, the Coromante had sliced his neck off so neatly that blood only gushed out when the two pieces of the body fell to the ground.

By that time, all four had already exited the hut into the darkness of the lands beyond the plantation, leaving one slave woman who also crept silently in the opposite direction – and safety – of the women's lodge, very glad to be rid of the nightly demands of a cruel sexual sadist.

CHAPTER EIGHT

MAROON COUNTRY – 1683

The dense green forests held both animal and human life. The green canopy of leaves spread like a roof overhead, in which a variety of large and small wild birds with beautifully coloured feathers flew, built nests and raised their young. Wild pigs, generations of those that sailed in the holds of Spanish ships to feed the settlers that came in search of Taino gold, ran through the undergrowth to escape the sharp spears that made them a tasty meal; the rat-like coney, frogs and mongoose whose sounds made music with the insects, large and small lizards – these were some of the forest inhabitants.

Men knew these forests too. The Taino had come first, the beautiful people who first peopled these islands living quietly on fish, coconuts and vegetables, worshiping gods of their own and trading with the other islands. Unable to co-exist with wave after wave of Spanish colonial settlers who forced them to dig for gold, they left their calm beaches and vegetable gardens to escape the predatory pale-skinned people, whose false embrace of friendship turned into forced and brutal labour.

Then the Black Moors brought from Spain, where they were renowned for their craft skills in metal and precious stones, also rebelled against the enslavement that was forced on them when they arrived in Jamaica and were the first to free themselves and run to the hidden mountain forest of trees and cockpit sinkholes to recreate the African jungle.

More took shelter there when the English captured the island in 1648 and thereafter imposed an even more cruel form of slavery on the humans they imported from Africa. These free people, and their descendants, were still there in the hidden hills, determined to live their own lives free from control by others, free to recreate the Africa from which they had been taken, in the country in which they now live.

The mountains were green and lush. The earth was brown and soft and good to grow food, there were coneys and wild pigs running in the forest, and plump birds in the trees and skies. Water flowed in clean streams spring from the rocks, and the leaves of the thatch palm trees covered the roofs of shelters.

*   *   *   *

Quamin walked up the almost-invisible track to the tree in which he had built their shelter and home. Vines had been woven between the thick branches to give shelter from the rain, and the thatch palm blended with the thick cover of leaves to provide a perfect home. Sheathing his machete in a looped belt at his waist, he hoisted himself easily up into the tree, using the branches quickly as steps. He reached a platform of leaves spread over a network of stout branches set to make a firm foundation.

He kissed Kofia, who waited for him there.

"Thank you for bring me back home to Africa," she said as they embraced.

"Thank you for being brave enough to join me," he replied. "This is our new land. We will make this land our Africa."

Quamin emptied his bag, bringing out bunches of wild berries, a large fruit like an orange and a bunch of fresh leaves. They ate the fruit, as Quamin opened his water gourd and they both drank.

"Are you content, my beloved?" he seemed anxious.

Kofia hugged him. "I am with you, so I am happy. We are not alone. The others who have given us shelter know how to survive in these forests. We will survive, Allah so wills it," she smiled.

"Tomorrow I will kill a wild pig and we will have more food."

"Pig is forbidden food!" Kofi was shocked.

But Quamin was serious. "You were forced to eat enough of it at the plantation, so why can't you eat it here? They run wild. Allah has sent all we need to survive!"

Quamin spread his arms wide. "Survival is all that is important now. We have almost forgotten our Koran prayers in this heathen land and still Allah has not abandoned us. Let us survive so we can fight to end this brutal British slavery. We are fighters now, warriors, and we will WIN!"

Kofi saw again what she loved in this man. This was the warrior she knew a man should be, a man like her father. This was HER warrior, the warrior whose woman she had been raised to be. She was proud to be his woman.

Now she will give him his children.

Their children.

Their African children.

*   *   *   *

In 1685 Kofia's first son was born. He was given the name Cudjo, after the day of the week on which he was born. Quamin had disappeared one dark night when her birth time was almost due, and returned early the next morning carrying a strange burden on his back. It was Old Nelly, the weary elder woman who had been whipped for being a 'healing woman' on the same day Kofia was.

Resting from the surprise of the strange journey that followed what should have been called a kidnapping, the old woman smiled up at Kofia with tears in her eyes:

"I had been praying to leave that place of evil for so long, but I had grown too old to try any more. Thank you for freeing me and may Allah Bless you! I am privileged to help you birth your child."

And so she did with the skills she had learned long ago in Africa from her mother and mother's mother, before being brought to the new land of pain and servitude. Now free, she was birthing the children of other Maroon women, performing the services of medicine woman to the people in the hideaway village where Kofia, Quamin and Ben Ahmed lived as free people. The community was growing, so were other groups of free people hidden away in the nearby hills and caves. They were glad to have someone who knew what leaves, roots and potions could heal wounds, fevers and injured limbs.

Africans had become bold in trying to sieze their freedoms. Slave rebellions sometimes resulted in as many as 600 freed people, many of whom were able to escape recapture and unite in the hidden cockpits as a rebel force to face the slave-owners' militia. Not afraid to raid the plantations, they boldly took weapons, powder and amunition in these assaults, as well as tools and useful items to make their new life more comfortable. Pots and pans were always a prize, as were machetes and pistols.

Their rebel communities grew into several small villages, some close to nearby plantations where slaves and free would gather on Saturday to sell and trade food both groups of Africans grew. Perhaps a pig would be exchanged for a good iron cauldron, or brooms for a strong leather belt from which to hang a sharp knife. There was an uneasy, but unspoken, truce between the two tribes, punctuated by jibes and teasing on both sides.

"Beautiful African queen, why don't you let me take you home to my Africa!"

Holding a tall walking stick as if it were a spear, the young free man puffed out his chest to show the shiny skin and rippling muscles, across which hung only a decorative string of large seeds and animal teeth -- a pair of breeches from a captured English soldier, his only clothing. He smiled gallantly at a shy slave girl lifting her long skirt out of the muddy earth, thick plaits shooting from under a floral bonnet, covering her smile under a shy hand but not before taking a sideways look at him.

"You coming?" he beckoned.

Before she could answer, another voice interrupted. "Come live with you wild men in the jungle? Why would a pretty girl like she want to do that for?" It was another, older slave woman who was shopping with the girl.

"To let snakes and insects bite up her skin and wild hog run her down? No sah. Massa take good care of us, we eat plenty food, sleep good at night. Massa soon catch all of you and bring you back to the plantation. I will watch you get beating."

With a look of contempt, she swept her skirt and the young girl away from the pile of bananas the Maroon sat beside.

But the girl looked back over her shoulder as she left.

The warrior smiled. "I will be coming for you!" he shouted.

*   *   *   *

On a rainy night in 1688, with the sky punctuated by lightning and thunder, Kofia's second child, her daughter BELLA was born. As the sky raged, the child made an equally turbulent entry into the world. Kofia smiled, as she kissed the baby Old Nelly placed on her breast. "Another woman to tell the Moon Secrets."

In 1690 Kofia's son Quaco was born, soon to grow as tall as his father and soon taller than his older brother Kodjo. Kofia helped Quamin grow all three children as Maroons in the hidden cockpits, learning the jungle life of the first generation of free Africans. It was a hard life for the adults, but for the children it was a gentle life to grow up in among adults who were happy despite the hardships to be living far away from their enslavers. They knew they would never see Africa again, so they would recreate it here in the island.

"The open areas of the community rang with the conversation of their women and the laughter of the children. Evenings found the children gathered by the older folk, where they were regaled with stories of the African homeland, of the prankster Anansi and of the wild animals and beasts which they would never see, except in their imaginations.

Heroic tales formed part of that activity and in this manner children were acquainted with the achievements of their ancestors and taught their obligations to the clan and to the family.

"Children were taught by their elders to be obedient and to respect authority. These were two of the skills to equip them for life. First, they learned the authority of the parent, and the older people in the community (age was revered). They were encouraged to respect those older than themselves and any such person could correct their wrong-doings. They knew who was their Chief, where the central power lay. They knew the elders and the community leaders. However, it was the tradition to withold from them certain specific details, until they were old enough to

understand the necessity to protect their cultural traditions. In this way the community operated much like a secret society.

"The children were taught bush survival; it was in the bush that they lived and itwas the bush on which they were dependent. Their elders and parents knew when they were ready for each progressive phase of development. It was not an issue left to chance, it was practiced and there were rules to which all adhered.

"Women were held in high esteem and the Maroon leaders frequently looked to them for leadership and direction, particularly when there were crises. Many of them accompanied the warriors out on their daring raids on the planters as well as on barracks and fortifications, distracting guards and carrying away the booty taken. So the women were mothers, wives, 'nurturers', farmers, culture carriers of the clan." [4]

Kofia's children learned to plant and care for food gardens planted with plantains, cassava and yams. They grew up helping the adults chop the hillsides footpaths in places where no solider could follow. They learned to disguise themselves with vines and branches to become

---

[4]   Ths History of the Maroons of Jamaica, Beverly Carey

invisible as they moved in the forests. And all three were taught by Quamin the battle tactics of stealth, discipline under orders and utter brutality, that gave the Maroons their fearsome reputation among the British soldiers that tried for nearly 100 years to subdue them and end their anti-slavery rebellion.

They learned, too, that even more afraid of the Maroon warriors than the British soldiers, were the plantation slaves forced to join their militia as bearers and sometime fighters who, knowing as Africans the cruelty and especially the secret powers they claimed to use to overcome an enemy, ran away before the battle began – some to join the rebels themselves.

*   *   *   *

1690

"We have new villagers," Quamin reported, returning from several days away, his machete covered with dried blood.

"Perkins estate," he reported. "One hundred of my Coromanti brothers rose up and set fire to the mill house .... the baracoons were left empty ... more than 60 ran away," He panted. "Twelve killed ... many recaptured, but not all of them. We fought as hard as we could to keep as many as we could … we probably have about 50 men with us, some women too."

"I wish we could have brought more!"

With roar of frustrated anger, Quamin flung his machete towards the thick trunk of a nearby tree, where it stuck deep and quivered for a moment before becoming still – the dried blood on it describing the battle more than words could.

"I tried!"

Kofia embraced him, as little Kodjo and Bella gathered round, hugging their father's strong legs that carried him safely back from his dangerous journey.

"You did well," Kofia conforted him. "I know they were glad you were there to help them fight. You are the bravest Maroon warrior, that is why you are our chief. You give us all the strength and direction to win our battles. You have not failed."

Kofia led him inside their shelter, a large round compound with thatched sides and roof. "You must be tired. Rest. I have made some sugar water for your return."

She gave him the large calabash and he drained it thirstily.

"Your hammock is waiting. Let me go see if I can help any of the newcomers settle in."

Kofia reached into the shelter for a large calabash, opened it and checked the leaves and roots inside. Then, leading a child with each hand, she set off into the darkness to other spaces she knew well in the hills where freed people lived, where her duty as wife of the Maroon Chief Quamin was to apply balm to wounds, reassure the escapees and find them shelter. Kofia did her work quietly, passing from one to another of the new arrivals.

She soon returned with news.

"Too many of the settlers soldiers are dying as they try to stop the runaways and the rebellions. They are planning to pass new laws to fight us. One of the new arrivals, a woman who served at table in the Perkins Great House, says they are going to pass new laws to prevent us free Africans from mixing and trading with the plantation Africans on their market day. They say we are influencing plantation Africans to run away, so they are going to make it illegal, then capture any free Africans who try to trade."

"Not good," Quamin snorted from his hammock. "We have been trading with the plantation Africans for years and such a law will prevent the plantation Africans from getting food they can't get on the plantation. Then again, the new settlers will need food before they establish their food gardens, they will need more than the clothes they ran away in, implements to till the soil and pots to cook the food they grow. It only means that we will have to make more raids on the plantations to get the things we need."

Kofia rocked the hammock lightly.

"They should give up their system of slavery and cruelty and let us be free to make our own lives, or choose to work for them for the right pay."

"Pay us!" Quamin snorted loudly. "They would never pay us! They only buy us! And brutalize us! We must wipe them OUT!!! We must keep fighting them until not one single slavemaster is left!!!"

"Ok. Be a little quiet now." Kofia cooled him with a fan of plaited coconut leaves. "Rest and sleep. Don't think about that now."

"I will organize a raiding party on the Gray's estate near Falmouth as soon as they stop looking for the Perkins runaways. They branded each of them, so it will be easy to identify they if they get caught." Quamin growled his anger.

"They can make all the laws they want!! Their laws are without teeth in the face of the Maroon steel and gunpowder! We are better warrior than they are!!! They can NEVER win!!!"

"You are a brave warrior, Quamin." Kofia spread herself across Quamin's chest. "I am filled with great feelings of joy when I consider you. Because of you, I can give thanks for the sufferings I have endured in my life, because they have all led me to your arms. Embrace me, my king. Give me your sweet nectar."

"You are the only sweet nectar, my beloved queen. I was born to belong to you, and you to me. Come, let us make another child." Quamin enfolded Kofia in his arms.

*　　*　　*　　*

CHAPTER NINE

MOON CHILD

"Mama! Mama! Kodjo is NOT being honourable!!!"

Bella came running towards her mother with a pout on her small face. At 14 years, she was long limbed like her father, and ran with a long stride using her spear-stick to keep her steps company. Her waist pouch weighed down her short skirt and her head was tied with a cloth that held shoulder length, thick plaits from her face.

Behind her, a playful smile on his face, ran her brother Kodjo. Though a year older, he was shorter in stature and wide-hipped like his mother. Around the waist of his breeches was slung a half-machete, its sharpened blade protected in a goatskin sheath. Garlanded around his chest and head were green vines that made him appear a moving shrub along the narrow path to the Maroon village. Behind Kodjo, laughing too was 10 year old Cofee using strong legs to keep company with the older children.

Kofia sat shelling peas on a tree stump stool outside the round thatch shelter that covered the cleared space under two large trees. Bella sat down beside her with an angry look.

"What's the matter now, Bella?" Kofia smiled as she embraced her daughter. "What have the boys been doing today?"

"Mama, Kodjo says I cannot play Leader of the Attack when we practice the Ambush war. He says I am just a girl, so I cannot. That is not true, is it Mama? Tell him it's not true!" Bella took a deep breath and grasped her arms firmly across her chest.

Kofia's face became serious and she answered quickly.

"You are quite right, my daughter. It is not true." She looked from Bella to Kodjo and Koffia.

"In our Africa, among the many women of a village there is always an important place for a woman as Leader. Just as a group of men needs a man as a Chief, an Army General, a High Priest, it also needs a Queen Mother, a Priestess and a Warrior Woman. To be a Mother is the work Allah ordains for woman. To be priestess is a duty she inherits by holy works; and to be Warrior Woman is to inspire the bravery of the Warriors she commands. And such a woman is respected as an equal, sometimes higher than even the Chief!"

"See! I told you so!" Bella turned to her brothers triumphantly.

"You must take turns with your sister to play Leader," Kofia explained.

"But I am older than her, and I am a man!" Kodjo frowned and folded his arms across his chest. "I am supposed to give the orders!"

"Not to me!" Bella stamped her foot. "I don't have to take your orders."

"So we will play without you, then!" Kodjo turned and ran back on the path into the bushes. Cuffee paused a moment, then followed him.

Bella stamped her foot again, then sat down angrily on the tree stump beside her mother's stool.

"Those boys! I wish I had different brothers to play with. That Kodjo is so proud that he has been chosen to be our father's successor. Since we were children our Father has taught all of us the wisdom and battle tactics that have kept us alive, all these years of war against the British colonials. I learned it just as well as he did. But because he is the eldest and a boy, he gets the honour on the sad day when our father makes his final sacrifice."

"Sometimes I wish I was born a boy!!!" Bella scratched the earth furiously with the end of her spear-stick.

Kofia smiled and put an arm around her.

"No, my daughter. Don't wish that. To be woman is to be more powerful than man can ever be!"

Bella looked at her mother curiously.

Kofia smiled. "Have you ever seen your mother as less than your father, except because she chooses to be humble before him?"

Bella smiled. "No, Mama. I see you live as equal partner with our Father and I see you endure the hidden life we live in the Cockpits, so I know you are a fiery, independent woman who inspires all the women who live among the Maroons!"

"This little incident with your brothers shows me it is time for us to have a very special talk." Bella waited for her mother to speak.

"My beautiful daughter, ever since you were born, each month when the full moon rises I have been teaching you the Moon Secrets that were taught to me when I was a young girl in Africa. I have taught you earth things like the seasons of rain and drought, the times of plantings of each of our important foods and how to cook them. You have been learning the sciences of the leaves and roots to be used as food and medicines and how to use them.

"From your father, you have learned to hunt a wild pig and skin a coney. Your father has taught you the war tactics that have kept us free Africans alive in these hills, and and you have become so brave that you have earned you the title of Warrior Woman. You have learned your lessons well. You remind me of the girl I was when they took me from Africa!"

Bella smiled at her mother.

"Since your monthly blood flow has now begun, I am going to start teaching you new lessons that will be the most important lessons you will learn as a woman. These are the Moon Secrets, the names of the heavenly lights, their meanings, destinations and how to align your actions in tune with the movements of these celestial magnets. This knowledge you will learn, combined with the knowledge you already have of earth and science, is a powerful mixture in a woman. If a certain special lesson is willingly added to what you already know, it will give you the ability to achieve whatever you want, win any battle, overcome any enemy, make any dream a reality."

"What is that, Mama? What other lesson can I learn?"

Kofia looked at her daughter seriously.

"You must learn to be a priestess."

Bella smiled with interest. "Ah! How do I learn that Mama?"

Kofia smiled with love. "It is a divine calling. You will hear a voice and you will follow the voice."

Bella continued to smile. "That sounds so strange, but interesting. What will his voice sound like?"

` Kofia's face grew serious.

"It will not be the voice of a man, Bella. In fact, you must be careful how you listen to the voice of ANY man."

Bella's eyes opened wide. "No man?"

"No, my beloved daughter. It will not be a man's voice. Follow only the angelic voice you hear. That voice will always direct your way."

"How ... when will I hear the voice?" Bella was puzzled.

"You will hear it."   Kofia hugged her daughter.

"Becoming a priestess is a big responsibility. Once you have reached that pinnacle, you cannot turn back. Going forward is the only way, but it is hard work with many sacrifices. You have to be sure you can endure to the end. You don't have to take that step, you can be content to be a Queen Mother for your community and that is still a good contribution to make. To be a priestess is a high and noble order with everlasting blessings. But you have to be sure, very sure, to take on the work of priestess."

Bella's face was serious.

"Teach me the lessons Mama. I will work hard."

Kofia smiled. "You are already learning. Your life has been your lessons. You have learnt the most important lesson, to know the difference between good and evil and you will always choose good. That is in you now, and you can't change even if the colonials were to capture you and lash you till your back till it looks like mine. You will never be evil. That is the first lesson. Once you know that, the foundation is there like these limestone rocks that cannot be moved"

With her finger, Bella marked the earth at her feet with some of the letters she had been learning with the other children in the communal afu-yard.

"Look Mama! These are the marks that mean Priestess. Am I right? Is that what I will become?" She pointed.

Kofia's eyes opened wide. She grabbed her daughter in a tight hug and, looking up to the dark night sky, let out her words in a whoosh of wind.

"MOTHER! YOU ARE HERE!" Kofia spoke to the heavens.

A little frightened at her mother's response, Bella asked. "What is it Mother? What did I do?"

With a wide smile, her mother answered: "You wrote it well,my daughter. You wrote our tribe's name for the greatest of our 'Priestesses. You wrote 'NANNA."

"Who was she? Tell me about her?" Bella was eager to know more.

Kofia smiled and looked admiringly as her daughter.

"In time you will find that you know her even better than I can ever tell you."

And with that puzzle Kofa began the next level of the secret Moon lessons.

CHAPTER TEN

FREEDOM PLANS

Bella quickly scraped out the last of the evening meal from the calabashes and turned them down without giving them too clean a wash. She tied her wrap cloth around her waist and hurried outside. She didn't want to miss a word the men were saying in the communal afu-yard, for their arrival had been a noisy sensation in the village, shouts of victory of a successful battle, some cries of pain from wounded warriors, the busy actions of women gathering and preparing food as the necks of chickens were wrung and hogs slit to be cooked over the fires smoking in front of each thatch-covered house.

Bella had helped Kofia preparing food, until her mother felt she could leave her to take care of cooking the rest of the meal, while she took her medicine bag over to where other women were caring for the wounded. Now everyone had eaten and the men were gathering around the smooth dirt circle of the Afu-yard.

Kofia had placed Quamin's seat outside the door of their house, a long curved slab of wood supported by an X-frame with a slanting back and polished arm rests. He sat on it like a king, and indeed he was. As chief of this village and strategic general of the free African warriors in this settlement of villages, the Coroman had long ago been acknowledged as Chief by all the African communities in the West of Jamaica. This was the largest settlement of free Africans on the island, though there were other settlements to the east of the island in St. Thomas and increasingly, in Portland.

The people who gathered around small fires in the bright moonlight were first and second generation free Africans who had run away from the cruel punishments of English enslavers, some singly, others in groups following uprisings on nearby plantations. For some, this was the first time they had arrived at a place that was not part of an Englishman's property. For others, they had been living in the free forests for many years. All were devoted to keeping their freedom to live and reconstruct a life as close as possible to that which had been left behind on the merciless slave ship journey. Some had battle-scars that were old and scarred, others shed fresh blood and winced with pain of wounds. All were battle-weary, but ready for whatever came next.

Bella came outside to rest on the ground beside her mother, who sat on the left side of Quamin's chair holding a calabash of sweet cane juice for him to sip occasionally. She watched the men gathering for the meeting to begin. She saw men as old and older than her father, and boys as young as her own sixteen years. They carried instruments of fire and steely death that they had won in encounters with English redcoats and that helped them secure their freedom. Some leaned on strong sticks as thick as their arms that served as weapons when necessary. Others still suffering the effects of the recent battle lay resting on the beds of palm leaves set on the ground or on wooden seats, their wounds wrapped in healing leaves and poultices and their faces grimly set to bear their pain.

As the gathering increased in numbers, Bella's brothers Kodjo and Cufee moved from the group of young men they had been speaking with and came to stand behind their father on his right side, holding their battle sticks like spears planted in the ground. Proud young warriors and heirs to Quamin's chieftainship.

Bella eased up from her stoop, went inside the house and returned with her own stout stick and took a new position standing on the left hand of her father. Kodjoe frowned, touched his father's shoulder, whispered a word and with a move of his head, made Koro turn to see his daughter. But rather than being upset, Quamin smiled to see her. And nodded, acknowledging her presence in warrior stance. Noting the interchange, Kofia smiled up at her daughter, nodding her approval.

Bella raised her chin. She knew the knowledge she had learned from her mother's Moon Secrets qualified her to stand as equal, a warrior woman.

Quamin clapped his hands, three loud claps, indicating the meeting was officially starting. An older woman stepped forward, the spirit medium who regularly conducted the night-long ceremonies and rituals through which the Africans connected with their ancestor spirits in drumbeat, dance and song that sprang from the country that had given them birth. Shaking a large calabash rattling with items only she could know, she shouted a prayer asking the spirit gods to bless the words and thoughts of all. Women in the gathering echoed her shout, while the men beat their chests and shouted the name of the Great Maker of All, the Omnipotent ALLAH!!!

In the still night, the cries of night owls, a deep rumble of thunder, followed by the whoosh of a strong wind, were the only sounds made by this human prayer.

That done, Quamin began.

"Welcome to all the brave warriors who have fought to free yourselves from the forced labour of the white slave masters. Your fight was glorious and the battle victorious. May your wounds heal quickly and may the bad memories of your enslavement vanish like smoke from our fires."

There was a murmur of approval, and he continued. "We welcome the men from Suttons to our homes. Make yourselves welcome. Be prepared to defend your freedom here as bravely as you did to come here. We who live here welcome your company. As our numbers increase, we become stronger to defend our freedom. We will teach you our ways of battle that have kept us free these years, free to plant gardens and grow children.

"The people who brought us to this island do not want us to live free, only want us to work for free. We would be happy to work for them for pay, but they are not like the masters we knew in Africa. Where we come from, slaves have rights, we can own property, and the child of a slave and the master becomes a free person. Owners are not allowed to murder their slaves unless permitted by the King, not like here where owners can do whatever they want to their slaves,and they think of the most cruel things to do!"

The men and women erupted in a thunder of noise, an avalanche of voices crying out in memory of some cruelty personally experienced, witnessed, of which they were still feeling the emotional and physical pain. Quamin let them express themselves, then signaled them to be still.

A man stood up and stepped forward into the clearing.

"On my estate, the master devised the wickedest punishment I ever saw. He made the drivers hold down an African who had said he was too sick to work that day and made another African empty his bowels into that man's mouth. Then he fixed on the mouth lock, screwed it shut around his neck and left him like that, lying on the ground!! The man could not do anything to spit it out, he just had to keep swallowing it!! You could hear him moaning in his throat, in his chest, in his heart. It was terrible to watch!!!"

The people were disturbed, disgusted, shocked as the story continued.

"It took him five days to die. The master just laughed and laughed and laughed."

The people were angry now, voices raised confirming stories of brutality and hatred, determined for vengeance, some roaring, some crying...

A middle-aged woman pushed through the crowd to the front of the cleared space and at the top of her voice shouted: "They strung up a pregnant woman by her hands in a tree and slit her belly so the baby fell out!!! Some of us women rushed out to catch the baby as the woman's blood flowed to the ground ... but the Massa whipped us back with his lash ... we had to watch and cry and throw ourselves on the ground."

In a flood of loud sobs, the woman threw herself on the ground and beat it with her fists.

Another man stepped forward,, took off his hat and held it to his chest.

"On my estate, the most terrible noise we would hear at night was the sound of our young boys being violated by the master. He like to choose them young and the more loudly they screamed, the more he liked his disgusting sexual relief. One boy was so sad at what was done to him, he threw himself into the sugar mill fire that he was carrying trash for. We were going to try and pull him out, but a wiser man said we should leave him as he was better off dead."

Quamin waited till the wave of noise and sorrow and anger stilled. Then he stretched out a hand.

"We can NEVER again live under such conditions, to be controlled by such devils. We will NEVER go back to that HELL Here we make life. Here we are safe. Here we are free. For now. We will have to fight to keep this freedom, but we will fight to the end, for it is all we have."

The gathering settled down with murmurs of agreement.

"You have brought word of plans the slave masters are making to capture and return us to their hell on earth. Who is your spokesman. Step forward!"

A man in his mid-thirties stepped forward. He carried his musket in his hand and a large pouch slung from his waist. His jacket had recently been on the back of an English soldier, though the red colour was now stained with both earth and blood. Over one eye he wore a patch of leather tied behind his ears.

"I am called 'Johnny' I disremember the name my mother gave me, I was captured when I was still a child. I served as butler in Massa Weston Harris household on the Pembroke Hill estate. I was quite happy there, until he punished me for nothing at all and put out my eye with a hot stick."

He raised the corner of the patch of leather, to show a blacked and inflamed hole where his eye should have been.

"It is still not healed completely, but I did not complain because I knew the other slaves were planning the rebellion. Everybody was tired of Massa Harris cruelty. I knew it was just time until I would to get my revenge. We cut off his head before we left in the night. Now we use his skull as a drinking bowl."

And from his pouch he pulled a skull bleached as white as its owner's skin had been!!

There was a gasp of shock and some horror as Johnny revealed his gruesome prize. But a laugh rang out, then another, and soon the whole gathering was convulsed with laughter, holding their bellies, leaning on one another for support, and the drummers beat their laughter into the drum-skins, making a joyous rhythm joining in the pace as Johnny danced around they yard holding the skull high and shouting for joy, till it became the center of a true celebration of happiness that relieved some of the sadness they all shared.

Bella stood wide-eyed as she listened to the tales of bitter enslavement. She looked with pride and gratitude at her father and mother, who had fought to raise her in freedom, never to experience those horrors, the pain and brutality of slavery. She gripped her stick more firmly and set her face strong, determined that she would never allow herself to be captured to experience the life they all had fought hard to escape from.

As the gathering quietened down, Johnny continued his story.

"Yes, he took one of my eyes, but I can see very well out of the other eye and I hear perfect out of both ears." The voices around him turned to silence.

"I've heard what the planters are planning. Brother Quamin, we will need your battle wisdom to stay ahead of them – to stay FREE!"

His voice swelled and, one after another, the crowd took up the cry!

FREE!!!   FREE!!!   FREEEEEEE!!!!!!

CHAPTER ELEVEN

HOW TO FLY

In 1696 the Jamaican legislature enacted a law "For the Better Order and Governing of Slaves". In 1699 one of the early party laws, entitled "An Act for Raising Parties to Suppress Rebellious and Runaway Negroes" was passed. Many such parties were drawn from the same areas where the Maroons had previously lived. The slaves who served in the militia were most probably known to the pre-Maroons from the estates where they belonged.

In 1702 another Act was passed "For the More Effectual Raising of Parties ot Pursue and Destroy Rebellious and Runaway Slaves". Similar acts either to form parties or to raise funds to support parties were enacted in 1705, 1706 and 1707. By 1713 it was evident that there was a serious problem in the east. A white planter was murdered by Africans located in the Buff Bay valley. Whereas in times [ast om the east, the planters possessions were under seige, it was feared that the Maroon threat was now extended to the person of the planter. Panic set in.

By 1718 the government concluded that the Maroon communities posed a serious threat to the overall security of the island. In 1722 this crystalized into the establishment of a special committee to consider the matter further. The committee sent in their recommendations to the House of Assembly and these were formalised in that same year in an "Act to Speed the Settlement of the North-East of the Island" which was passed.

The thought was that if the coastal areas around what is now Port Antonio were settled, the Maroons would in time be forced to restrict themselves to the mountains. The new Parish was to be called Portland after the new Governor, the Duke of Portland. A town was to be established on the peninsula and this was to be called Titchfield, after another of the Duke's lesser titles.

The panic of the planters was exacerbated and order and control would not be achieved until after Major General Hunter arrived in Jamaica in January 1929. at that time the 'first time' or original Maroons had been living for centuries in the area which had been selected to be the new parish of Portland, but the plans afoot for its

*conversion into a dense settlement of English planter
families were not in the interest of the Maroons.*

*By the time that Hunter arrived. African settlements
had considerably increased al over the southern slopes of
the Blue Mountains. Unfortunately, his tenure saw the
already poor relationship between all the inhabitants
deteriorate further and create the conditions for what
would become known as The First Maroon War.*[5]

*   *   *   *

"Tonight's lesson is learning how to fly!"

Bella was by now used to being surprised by the Moon
Secret lessons she received from her mother each time the
moon was full. Sitting with her mother under the bright
silver light, she would listen to the stories from the country
her mother said she used to live. She would hear how to heal
wounds by the touch of a special leaf, how to make a coney
or a wild pig freeze in its tracks to be captured without
bloodshed, how to blow ashes into special clouds to bring
rain.

---

[5] The Maroon Story: The Authentic and original History of the Maroons
in the History of Jamaica 1490-1880: Bev Carey; Agouti Press,, 1997

Her mother had taught her how to disappear from sight, not only by covering herself with branches and leaves like the warriors did to attack the white soldiers by surprise, but how to vanish from sight as if she simply did not exist. Her mother was a good teacher of that particular skill. Bella remembers how she bawled the first time her mother did that. "Mama! Mama!" she had cried out, till she was stunned into silence when her mother materialized before her eyes.

Bella had jumped into her arms and hugged her tight. "Don't do that again, Mama! You frightened me!!! But show me how to do that!" And Kofia did.

But to fly! Surely that was not possible.

"It is not difficult. You have seen the birds do it. And the rats that fly by night. You can do it." Kofia insisted.

"How Mama?"

"It is simple. You must study the incantation, the words you must speak to make you light enough to fly. Learn the words by heart and then you must practise, and you will be able to fly."

"Tell me the words mother. I have always wanted to fly, to see the earth like the birds to from high up! Tell me the words!"

Kofia cupped her hands around Bella's face behind her ears, pressed her face to her daughter's and whispered. Once. Twice. Three times.

"Lean the words by heart until you need them. I will ask you again next Moon time."

The words echoed in Bella's head, repeating themselves over and over. She was certain she would remember them. Bella smiled at the idea of flying like a butterfly or visiting a flower like a bee, repeating the words softly, over and over as she lay in her hammock. She was eager to put the lesson in action. Early the next morning Bella tied on her wrap, picked up her stick and headed into the forest. She knew a ledge in the limestone rock that would be a good place to fly from, and she was going to try.

The morning was bright, but not yet hot. The thick forest shaded the bright red earth beneath Bella's feet as she trod the beaten path that led from the village. Birds filled the silence with their musical cries, sweeping through the branches in singles, pairs and flocks. Dew still rested on the leaves and Bella stopped to drink some water settled in the cupped leaves out of which a tree orchid bloomed. A small bird with iridiscent blue feathers and a long tail darted off its morning sip from a flower's nectar and Bella smiled.

"I am coming to join you," she whispered to the bird.

Soon she was at the ledge, an outcrop of white rock that jutted out over the valley giving a wide view of the mounds of tree-covered rocks that covered the earth like massive upturned cups of green. On the far horizon Bella could see smoke from a plantation's sugar millhouse. It was reaping time and the smoke would not cease until all the sugar was juiced, boiled and made into sugar and molasses. The freed Africans told tales of horror about the sugar mill-house with its treadmill, the fire that must constantly be fed, and the brutal beatings which were administered at the slightest pretext.

"I will fly over and take a look at the mill-house," Bella thought to herself. She knew nothing of life on a sugar plantation and she was glad because she knew the price to be paid by all who had such knowledge. But sometimes, especially when warriors brought special things back from raids on nearby estates – a bolt of shiny satin fabric, a gold-rimmed mirror, a finely carved table -- she wondered what that life was really like.

"Yes." Bella was confident. She felt wise, strong, a warrior woman free to live as she chose, do as she wished.

"Now that I know how to fly, I will go and take a look for myself."

Bella laid down her stick, planted her feet firmly on the edge of the cliff, and uttered the incantation she had memorized all night.

"Holy Mother, Divine Father. Hear my voice.

O angel wings, unfold. Spread out! Lift me up!

Let me rise on the wind! Let me fly with the birds.

I am ready. UP! UP! UP! I FLY!!!"

Bella spread out her arms, closed her eyes and jumped into the air.

The next thing she knew was that she was bumping up and down slung over a man's shoulder. A strong arm was holding her at the waist and her head was facing the ground behind him as he walked quickly through the forest. There was a lot of pain. Bella moaned, then cried out.

"What ... who..."

The arm released her and lifted her gently to lie on the ground. The man's voice was strong and angry.

"What were you doing? Why did you jump? Do you want to kill yourself?"

It was Johnny, the one-eyed man. "Your arm is broken. I found you in the forest. I am taking you back to the village. Your mother will take care of you. What were you doing?"

He reached for his goatskin water bag and put it to Bella's lips. She sucked a mouthful of water from the opening. Her teeth felt shaky and her head was reeling.

"I was flying." was all she could say.

"You were flying!!! You are mad!!! You just fell out of the sky into the trees! People can't fly, only birds!" Johnny was shocked.

"Mama says people can fly." Tears came to Bella's eyes. "Mama says so."

"Just rest a little. You are badly hurt. I will take you home to your mother. I hope you are not too big for her to punish you for telling lies. People can't fly."

Bella looked at him. "Mama will explain everything. Thank you for helping me."

"Let me tie up your arm. It needs a splint."

Removing his machete from his waist, he chopped a firm branch from a nearby tree, then pulled down some vines that draped the branches. Holding the branch against Bella's arm, he tied it around with the vines then used another vine to make a sling around her neck for her arm.

"How does that feel? A little better?" Bella nodded. "Come, let us continue."

Lifting her up with strong arms and holding her like a baby, he set off again along a familiar path towards the village.

Soon they reached the plantain walk with its acres of bearing trees that marked the outskirts of the village. People weeding the vegetable fields stopped and rushed to help Johnny carry Bella the last few steps, while a woman ran ahead of them calling to Kofia.

"Come, Come! Your daughter is hurt! Come!"

Kofia rushed towards the crowd now gathering around Bella and Johnny.

"Bella, what happened to you? Did you meet up with soldiers? How did you get hurt?"

Bella looked at Johnny and placed a finger to her lips. Kofia saw the sign and led Johnny to carry Bella inside their house and lay her down comfortably. Then, draping a cloth over the entrance to avoid prying eyes, she knelt by her daughter's side and mopped her forehead with a cloth dipped in water.

"Mama, I was trying to fly. Tell this man that people can fly. Tell him Mama."

"Oh, Allah be praised!!! I see what happened. You were trying to fly!" Koria was shocked. "Girl, you are lucky you are not dead! It takes more than one night to learn how to fly! You must believe and believe and believe until you will do it without even thinking."

Kofia smiled, as she unwound the vine from around Bella's neck and reached for her medicine bag.

"And you must not try the first time by yourself. You can see why." She gave Bella a leaf to chew.

"Chew this. A fever is going to rise in your body while the medicine in the leaf heals you. Lie still and rest. It will take a few days before the pain is gone, and weeks before your arm can use your stick again." Kofia placed two new leaves on Bella's forehead that would reduce the pain that was beginning to sweep over Bella's body.

She turned to Johnny. "You saved my daughter. Thank you. She could have laid there all day and died from loss of blood! You have one eye, but two hearts."

Johnny held down his head with modesty.

"And you made a good brace for her arm. I will leave it in place. Thank you again.".

Johnny smiled. "I am glad I was there."

"I need another favour, Johnny," Kofia looked deep into Johnny's good eye.

"Please don't tell anyone about the flying. Keep it our secret. Not everything is good to tell."

"Ok Nana Kofia. I will keep the secret. I know people can't fly. Children have such strange ideas."

"I am not a child! Mama says people can fly!" Bella raised herself up and spoke strongly, but the effort weakened her and she lay back.

"Hush girl, just rest now." She turned to Johnny. "I can never thank you enough. I am indebted to you for saving my daughter's life. Is there something I can give you as reward. You can have any of Quamin's rifles or swords, or any food you need in your house, anything ..."

Johnny smiled and bowed to both women. "If what Bella says is true that people can fly, I would like to learn how. Can you please teach me. That would be a great reward."

Kofia paused, but realized Johnny had earned the right to ask any favour of the person whose life he had saved. She sighed deeply.

"Alright, I will teach you how, but don't let that be an excuse to visit Bella when I am not here. Otherwise, the door will be closed."

'I understand, Nana. I understand. Thank you."

CHAPTER TWELVE

WAR DANCING

It was the first war dance Bella had ever seen and she looked with awe at the spectacle before her. Bathed in the bright silver light of the full moon all the villagers of their mountain hideout, more than 50 persons, as well as another 40 persons who had traveled from near and far encampments of self-freed Africans, had come together for tonight's ceremony.

Dressed as if for war, their clothes looked like armour, made of strong canvas, goatskin and leather that protected and covered their bodies. Tied around their heads and plaited into their hair were leafy branches that made their movements look like a small forest in motion.

In their hands they carried metal-tipped spears, sharp machetes, a few rifles, some muskets and many stout sticks.

Four drummers kept up a rhythm, two on small drums held between their knees, one on a goatskin that covered a thick slice of a giant hollowed tree trunk,, and one pounding a stick on a large calabash. The rhythm of the drums accompanied the many pairs of feet that marched counter-clockwise around a fire that burned in the center of the Afu Yard, it's light adding to the moon's illumination and making the space as bright as day.

Quamin and Kofia sat on high stools, King and Queen of the Western Africans. On their heads were tall crowns of plaited palm fronds interlaced with leaves and bright flowers of hibiscus and wild ginger. Around Kofia's neck hung a string of pieces of broken coloured glass that glistened in the light. In his hand Quamin held the sacred Abeng that had called them all here to the War Dance. The flecks of gray in his hair and beard were as much marks of pride in his survival, as were the battle scars on his arms and chest, bare except for a leather strap that held the scabbard for his large and shiny machete.

Bella watched the the throng of marchers. Their slow steps echoed the long march of a long line of chained people taken from their villages to the slave ports on the African coast, to the ships, to the brutal, miserable, inhuman journey and to their enslavement in this small country. Yes, it was the same march, and many of those marching were reliving the same memories with their steps.

The memories of those journeys brought from them songs that made them moan, cry out in pain, shout to heaven to gods of strange names, as they shuffled around in the circle. One song marched around the fire for many rounds, then it was replaced by another, then another, an endless supply of voices in harmony with one purpose. The songs they were singing in many verses of many languages had one sound only, the sound of their hearts, the pain of their memories of families lost, of brutality suffered, and of dreams left behind in the land from which they had been taken.

A woman screamed, then started whirling in mad circles, bumping into other marchers, falling on the ground, tearing off her clothes. Other women grabbed her, held her, tried to calm her as she shook in a trance, screaming some strange gibberish at the top of her voice. The other marchers paid her no mind, continued their sombre march and sang their mournful songs as if she was not there.

Another woman fell into the same trance, screaming, climbing up a tree with the agility of a monkey, then when rescued, pawing the ground on all fours like an angry beast, while two strong men held her down.

Bella was anxious. She leant over to Kofia. "Mother...?

But Kofia simply held a finger to her lips. "Watch and listen, daughter."

A third woman fell to the ground and started speaking in a gutteral growling voice.

"Ah. She has come." said Kofia so softly Bella barely heard her.

Kofia stood up regally and watched the gyrations of the third woman. Hands reached out to the woman, but Kofia stopped them with an outstretched hand. She stepped forward to stand in front of the drummers, bu-du-dup and with her feet she tapped out a faster rhythm on the ground. The drummers followed her lead and the drum beat got faster like a galloping horse. Bu-du-dup, bu-du-dup! U-du-dup!

The woman on the ground was still making noises, but now the tenor of her voice changed to a high pitch, the sound of a bird squawking loudly. Kofia signaled the marchers to stop the circle, so they stood and marched on the spot, pounding it under their feet in the same galloping rhythm as the drums.

The woman on the ground screamed loudly!

The drummers, the marchers, Kofia, all stopped, shocked silent by that scream.

And in that silence, an owl flew over the fire and was sucked down into it, its burning feathers sending a bitter smell into the smoke and the night.

Kofia knelt down beside the woman on the ground and lifted up her face to look directly into her eyes.

"Give us the message Kumba Najaai. We are listening!"

The face of the woman on the ground was unrecognizable, swollen and contorted in an ugly mask, eyes wide open and bulging, tongue hanging out of swollen lips. Bella turned her face in disgust, but her mother was still staring into the woman's face with no disgust. Her voice was strong and loud.

"GIVE US THE MESSAGE. WE HAVE COME TO HEAR IT."

Out of the swollen lips, with saliva dripping from the corners, the voice spoke. It was no language Bella had ever heard. It sounded like a rushing wind, like falling stones, like branches breaking. Bella heard the roar of animal and the cry of a dying bird in the sounds that came from the woman's mouth. All through it Kofia held the woman's face, looking straight into the woman's eyes, locked in combat with a spirit that tried, but failed, to conquer the moment and destroy whoever had penetrated into that dark space.

Then, just as suddenly, the woman collapsed, falling unconscious to the ground. Bella noticed that the other two women had also come out of their trances and were being comforted by companions.

Kofia stood up and signaled the drummers to begin again. She returned to her seat beside Quamin and spoke softly into his ear. Quamin's brow showed furrows of disappointment as she spoke. Then he stood up to address the gathering.

"You all know why we have come here tonight. There is talk of war. The planters are gathering an army together and this time they are using the enslaved Africans to swell their army. We are going to have to fight our own brothers this time and the war is going to be more bitter, more strong, more difficult than ever before.

"We have summoned the oracle to guide us and to assure us of victory. You have seen the oracle appear and you have heard him speak. He does not bring good news."

There was a murmuring among the people. One voice shouted: "War is never good news!"

Quamin continued. "The oracle says many will die." He paused for them consider his words. But the oracle also says their deaths will bring new life. I don't know what that means yet, but we must prepare for war, and for death."

The drummers beat a roll of thunder with their hands and the warriors jumped to the beat, shouting war cries. "We are ready for war."

"Oh we certainly are ready." Quamin beat his chest. "For us, our life has only one end, death. Whether it comes as old men, or as young warriors, death will come. I prefer to meet death as a warrior. I prefer to meet death killing a man who will deprive me of my freedom, for my freedom is my LIFE!"

The warriors roared their agreement. "You are our leader, Quamin. We are ready to follow you!" shouted one.

Another made a shout: "FREEDOM OR DEATH!" and it was taken up by 100 strong voices: "FREEDOM OR DEATH! FREEDOM OR DEATH! FREEDOM OR DEATH!"

Quamain quieted them "Thank you for your loyalty and support. I am humbly honoured to lead this battle. I am appointing my son Kodjo as my chief lieutenant. He has grown up learning about battle from me, and I know he is a trusty fighter and battle strategist. Many of you have seen him grow from a child and know that he is a loyal and true African. Please welcome him to his assignment. I know he will be a great warrior." He stretched his hand to bring Kodjo out of the crowd to stand beside him.

The roar of agreement that followed made Quamin and Cuffee smile. Kofia sent a nod of approval to them both from her high seat and the drummers started playing happy music for the celebration that had begun.

But Bella was not so sure. She turned to walk away from the boisterousness and find a quiet place, but instead she found Johnny blocking her path. He smiled.

"You are not happy with that, are you Bella?"

Bella was startled and shocked at his insight. "What do you mean?"

"I saw your face. You are not happy with your father's appointment. And I have seen enough of Kodjo while I have been living here to know that he is not as good a person as people think."

Bella didn't want to speak and tried to pass him, but he blocked her with a smile.

"Also, I think I would be just as good a chief lieutenant as him, I have even more battle experience than he does. You know that."

Bella looked down, then spoke. "Johnny, you are a good man, but I could never betray my own brother by agreeing with you."

"That is true and you are a royal woman Bella. Never mind what I said, I meant no offence. Johnny is here to serve you, respect you and protect you. That is all. Remember that." And with one step he vanished into the moonlit bushes.

Bella felt a rush of emotions ripple through her body that made her feel a little weak, not steady on her legs.

Grasping hard on her stick, she took a long, deep breath that enveloped the smells of the forest, then took another, and another. She thought about what had just happened. Why did that man cause such a reaction in her? What were those feelings that enveloped her as he spoke? Bella had never felt them before.

She stood there, thinking about all that had happened earlier in the night, the War Dance in the full moonlight ... the women who behaved like they were mad ... the appointment of Kodjo ... Johnny's conversation with her. This was Moon Secrets lessons night and there were more Secrets to learn this Moon night.

Bella felt her strength return to her body. Using her stick for balance, she took firm steps that soon brought her back to the yard, where people were still dancing to the drum beats and enjoying the night together. Someone had shared a keg of rum, distilled from sugar with slave labour and liberated from a nearby estate, and the liquor had made several people merry.

Bella found her mother still seated on her high stool beside Quamin. She realized that they would remain there all night until the white rooster tied by one foot to a nearby bush uttered his first high-pitched scream at the first sight of daylight, and the bloody severing of its neck thereafter signaled the end of the ceremony. Bella realized that to sit beside her mother through the night was part of the Moon Secrets she would learn that night. She sat on the ground beside Kofia.

"Can I bring you some water, Mama?" Bella asked.

"No, daughter. I must not eat or drink till dawn."

"Can we talk then?"

"You have questions, I know."

"Yes Mama. ... who was that woman and what did she say?"

Kofia lifted her chin up, her face emotionless, serious, shining like a polished ebony carving in the moonlight. She thought a while before she answered her daughter.

"You must see all three women, then you can see the answer. All three women were part of one message from the spirit gods. We called the spirit gods here with the drums and with our voices to guide us, advise us, give us wisdom, give us strength. They felt our steps pounding on the earth and they heard the beat of our hearts in the drumbeats and they heard the cries of our songs. The spirit gods came to us in those three women."

"If the spirit gods are good like you teach me, why did they come like that?"

"The spirit gods don't like to come to earth, my daughter. The earth is polluted by the bloody crimes of people on earth. Their crimes hide the beautiful earth that the spirit gods have created. So they don't want to come here when we call them, especially as they have to take on a human form to come here. They fight, they get angry and behave bad, try to kill themselves when we make them come back to earth, except they can't die, which makes them even more angry."

Bella nodded with understanding.

Kofia continued teaching.

"When we call the spirit gods, they send a messenger to see who called them. When that messenger does not return because the people who called them are holding them strong with the drums and the songs and the stepping, then they send a second messenger to see why the first has not returned.

"When they see that two messengers have not returned, the spirit gods realize they have to obey the wishes of those who called them, so that is when the true messenger comes. You have to know how to ignore the disturbing way the first two messengers are behaving and to wait for the third messenger before the message comes.

"Then you have to be prepared to look the messenger in the eyes and ask them to deliver the message. That is the hard part, for the messenger makes itself very ugly to trick you and keep you from receiving the message."

"How did you understand what she was saying?"

Kofia turned her face upwards to the moon, remembering times past.

"In our Motherland village, some women are born with an inner sight to speak with and hear messages from the spirit gods. In our village such women are respected and highly honoured because they hold such a special gift. It is a gift that comes to those who learn the Moon Secrets to become not just a warrior queen but a Priestess of the highest order. My mother passed the gift to me in her Moon Secrets, the science of the powers of heaven and earth. I am teaching you all the lessons you will need to speak with the spirit gods when your people need them."

"My people?" Bella was surprised. "These are not my people, they have you Mama."

"One day soon you will be queen of a village like this, Bella. On that day you will no longer be called Bella, but by your title as warrior priestess Nanna – she who speaks with the Spirit Gods. Get ready. You have been prepared for that position."

"What was the message?" Bella wanted to know.

A frown ruffled Kofia's forehead and she bent her head down.

"The messenger says we will win the battle that is before us. But some of us will die, many of us." Kofia's face showed pain and she looked sad. But then she shook her head and raised her face again. "I can't tell you any more of the message."

Bella took a deep breath, ready to speak, but Kofia reached her arm sideways and patted her daughter.

"No more questions. Sit silent now, and keep watch with me till morning. I must listen to the night."

"Anything you ask, Mama."

"I love you, my precious daughter."

CHAPTER THIRTEEN

MAROON WAR

"Make me brave... Make me strong... Make me victorious....make me brave... Make me strong... Make me victorious..."

Bella repeated the mantra over and over. She remembered the words her mother Kofia had taught her, the words that had carried her through her capture, her sea journey, her enslavement and her eventual freedom, and which her mother had promised would carry her safely through the battle to come.

Bella had helped her mother pack up their belongings the day before, emptying the small thatched house of all moveable, valuable possessions wrapped up in the hammocks, large strips of canvas clothing and bags.

From early morning the older women and children had set out carrying the village on their heads, a longline of people climbing up higher and higher into the hills of the

Blue Mountains, moving silent and invisible in the dense forest along paths that had been laid out as escape routes long ago when the village was first settled. There they had already built some similar little houses for an emergency like this.

Kofia said goodbye to her daughter, joining the older women. She would be needed to tend for the wounded who would be brought to the new hillside abode.

"Your first battle, my daughter." Kofie held Bella's shoulders tight.

"Fight well! Defend our freedom! Take blood!"

Bella looked deep into her mother's eyes.

"At last I get to fight a battle. My father and you have taught me well. I will defend our freedom to death!"

Bella watched her mother turn and join the climbers, following the sight of her back until it disappeared. Then it was time for her to join the warriors she was leading, a team of men and women armed with sharp machetes.

"Make me brave... Make me strong... Make me victorious....make me brave... Make me strong... Make me victorious..."

Bella repeated the mantra. She heard the first abeng sound the message that the enemy had been sighted. advancing on the edge of the nearest estate. It had begun. Now she would know what a real battle was like. Now she was no longer just a woman, but a Warrior woman.

The battle had been divided into four main stages. The invading army would soon meet the first stage of battle, the pits with sharp bamboo sticks that had been dug and hidden in the main path that led so innocently towards the village. The first stage captured and injured many of the first wave of soldiers, reducing their numbers and putting fear into the hearts of the slaves that accompanied them.

Bella was in charge of the second stage of battle and it was time for her warriors to take their position. Dressed in vines and tree branches, they slipped into the bushes along the side of a narrow path that ran along a mountain that dropped off into a precipice. Once they settled, Bella's warriors became part of the forest itself.

The army of soldiers dressed in red uniforms that were sorely inappropriate for the terrain in which they fought, marched past Bella and her warriors without seeing them. Bella counted more than 120 armed men who she let pass without harm. Twelve Africans followed, plantation slaves who had been forced to carry arms, or who were willing bearers. Four other slaves followed them carrying the army's food and arms.

"Make me brave... Make me strong... Make me victorious....make me brave... Make me strong... Make me victorious..."

Bella took the first blood. A tree branch became a hand carrying a sharp knife that severed a head from a body, Another strong branch threw both over the precipice. Bella's warriors were glad to follow her example. The earth of the man-made forest became wet with blood.

Seeing Bella's arm at momentary rest from relentless slaughter, one slave turned pitiful eyes to the eyes in the tree and begged for "Mercy!"

"Join us or die?" Bella whispered between clenched teeth.

"Allah be praised!" was his only sound.

"Take him prisoner," Bella ordered. "Let him live to tell the tale."

One by one, the slaves disappeared from the colonial army line, the sound of bodies falling into the jungle muffled by the dense a mass of branches they fell into, hardly disturbing the noise of soldiers marching ahead. The pile of captured booty left behind was high. Bella sent some of her warriors to take the captured guns and ammunition on another path over the hill to the warriors at the second battle point, Then she raised the abeng to her lips to signal the success of her battle and blew the message sounds.

Bella could hear another abeng take up the signal as the third battle began. As the path levelled into a clearing, the RedCoats were engulfed by a strong battalion of free Africans surrounding them with guns, muskets and hand-to-hand combat with machetes. As Bella and her warriors held their position, she could hear shouts and cries in English and in African languages that filled the day with the agonies of battle.

Bella heard the English general sound the retreat on his silver horn, telling his soldiers to escape down the hillside to the river. And Bella heard the abeng blower in the valley below send the signal to the warriors at the fourth battle point. Bella knew the battle was over now, because Quamin had expected the retreat and planned for it. Down in the valley beside the river that the English thought would rescue their retreat, Quamin and his soldiers awaited them with the fiercest battle of all. None would escape.

Bella gathered the rest of her warriors beside her. They stripped off the branches and vines of their disguise and picked up the weapons they had brought with them, and some new ones captured. Bella picked up two large empty musket shells from the path and pushed one on each of her wrists, holding them up with a smile to admire their shine. They would be useful in the next battle. Bella liked the smell of blood around her. It was a rich perfume that she would never tire of.

"I am a warrior woman now." Bella was proud of herself, and of her warriors.

"Come let us go down to the river," she signaled them to follow her. "The others will need help carrying the wounded up to the new place of rest."

Assigning one warrior to take charge of their captive, Bella led her warriors down the hill towards the river. Already a line of wounded was coming towards them through the trees, brave warriors who knew the price of freedom was bought with blood. The unwounded supported the walking wounded, they carried some over strong shoulders or on their backs, or on makeshift stretchers of tree limbs around which vines had been wound.

Bella had seen such a line of men and women after a battle, for it was to her mother Kofia and the medicine women of her company, but something was wrong. In times after other battles the warriors faces would brighten when they saw Bella, knowing that she was as adept at the healing sciences as her mother who had taught her. But this time the warriors cast their eyes down when they saw Bella. One turned his face away, the face of another had tears. Bella soon saw why.

Coming towards her was a stretcher carried by two men, Johnny leading at the front. As they saw her, he shouted: "Keep her back! Don't let her see this!"

It was too late. With a swift leap Bella was beside the stretcher.

It was Quamin.

"Oh NO!!!" My father!" Bella signaled the bearers to stop and lay Quamin on the ground.

"Where is he hurt?"

The wound was a gaping hole of blood and flesh that seemed to completely cover the left side of Quamin's chest.

"Our chief, your father, fought bravely at the front of our warriors," Johnny spoke softly. "He said it was his right to take the life of the army captain who had brought soldiers to take away our freedom. Our chief attacked him face-to-face and chopped him, severed the man's left arm. But the man shot him full on with his musket. It hit our Chief, but he did not fall, he did not fall until he had severed the man's head from his body in one clean chop."

Bella's tears flowed down her face.

Quamin opened his eyes. They were red, burning like a fire was burning in them.

"The spirit gods have blessed us with victory, my daughter. We are safe again."

Quamin's eyes closed, his chest still moved beneath the gore and blood.

"I am glad, my father. Victory is yours."

Bella wiped the tears from her face. This was not the place or time to cry. She was a warrior woman now. She must find her mother and help her. She turned back up the hill and, moving swiftly, soon passed the bearers and headed through the trees to the place where a new village was already being established.

At the top of the hill stood a giant cotton tree supported by several massive roots that rose up out of the ground thick like walls. These sheltered roots that had become the hospital for wounded warriors. In each fold of the roots healers tended to their wounds under the supervision of Kofia as, one by one, the wounded were brought to be cared for.

Bella reached her mother, hoping to be the first to give her the sad news, but she realized that word had already reached Kofia of Quamin's wound for Bella could see that her mother had also shed some tears. But she knew not to mention it or to shed any tears of her own for her mother to see.

"Come my daughter," Kofia embraced Bella. "Let us get ready to heal your father."

Leaving the other healers, Kofia made one fold of the roots into a private space, spreading a pile of branches, then laying a cloth over them to await Quamin. As she waited, she scattered powder over the space, took special roots from her medicine bag and placed them around the sides of the cloth, then knelt down. Holding her head up to the sky, Kofia spoke special words to the spirit Gods.

"Come Spirit Gods of healing! Bless this place! Restore flesh! Replace blood! Give LIFE!"

Bella knelt beside her mother and listened to her words. Silently she spoke to the spirit gods herself.

"Spirit gods, don't take my father from me. Cover his wound. Bring back his life! Show me your powers!"

With no one to see, Bella let her tears fall. She had not considered the thought of her father being wounded or dyding. He had seen him return from many battles, recover from many wounds – the worst of which came not from battle but from hot pursuit of a wild pig that turned and gored his right leg so badly he was laid up for a month unable to stand on a pus-infected leg.

This was unexpected, and from the sight of the wound, Bella could see it was serious. Soon enough the bearers brought Quamin to the cotton tree and laid him to rest on the bed Kofia had prepared. A crowd of villagers gathered round, but Kofia did not want them around.

"I will take care of our Chief. Go, help the others. Help build the new village, There is much work to be done."

Only the children Kodjo, Bella and Quako were allowed to keep watch over Quamin as Kofia worked. From the small fire she had made, Kofia singed some thick cactus leaves till the gell turned brown, then placed them on Quamin's wound. He flinched at the pain, then fell back unconscious again. His breath came hard and long, dug up from a deep place beneath his wound. His body trembled, then heaved.

Kofia signalled her sons to help hold their father down. One on each side, they held his arms, placed their weight on his strong, muscled legs, and held him firm till the spasms subsided.

Kofia gave Bella a wet cloth to hold on her father's head. Quamin felt so hot, Bella could feel the heat through the cloth. She dipped it in the calabash of water, and placed it again, and again. If that was all she could do for her father, Balla was glad to do it.

*   *   *   *   *

Bella woke with a start and sat up sharply. Looking around, she saw that she had fallen asleep beside her father, tucked in beside his warm body as she used to as a child, with her hand still holding a cloth on Quamin's forehead. Now fully awake, the events of the previous day came back forcefully – the battle, the blood and the final sorrow of her father's wound.

She looked around. Her mother Kofia sat on a stool at Quamin's head. In her hand she held a bundle of herbs that were burning slowly and sending out a spicy, earthy smell. Bella could see her mother had not slept all night, keeping watch over Quamin. Kofia's lips moved silently, speaking a continuous conversation with the spirit gods, asking healing and life for her beloved Quamin.

Bella stepped out of the fold of tree roots that sheltered Quamin and found herself face to face with Johnny.

"How is Chief Quamin?"

"He is sleeping." Bella was glad to see him.

"Were you here all night?"

"Yes." Johnny stamped his spear stick into the ground and threw back his chest. "I will wait right here day and night until our Chief recovers. I will not leave his side."

"Neither will I!" Kofia was defiant. "You can go now and take your rest! My brothers and I can take care of our father!"

"Oh yes?" Johnny smiled. "Where are Kodjo and Quako?" Bella looked around her, shocked that neither were around.

"They are sleeping." Johnny was scornful. "They are with their women making new children!! You are the only one who cares. You are the only true warrior of all Chief Quamin's children!"

Bella was silent. She could not speak while she considered Johnny's words.

"I have told you once before." Johnny insisted. "I am here to protect you and respect you. I will take care of you. And I will take care of your father."

Bella held down her head. This man was determined. It was good to have a trusted friend. And Johnny was known as a good warrior.

"Thank you Johnny." Bella felt tired, tired of being strong. She wished she could rest.

"You need to rest," Johnny spoke softly. "Soon your body will start to ache after all the work of the battle yesterday." Bella could feel her arms muscles aching. Johnny was right.

"Go take a bath in the river and wash the battle off your body. Get fresh, then come back to sit with your father and help your mother. She will be glad of your help."

Bella looked at him. How did he know how she felt, what she needed? She was suddenly filled with a strong inner warmth of gladness that, for a moment, wiped away the pain and sorrow she was feeling. How could a man's words make her feel so strange, so happy, so wanting to rest in his strength, his warmth, his comfort?

Bella turned and rushed down the hillside. Yes, The river would be cool, refreshing. No, she could not let those feelings she did not understand overwhelm her. She was strong, she was invincible, she was Warrior Woman.

*　　　*　　　*　　　*

CHAPTER FOURTEEN

WE WILL FLY

The drums beat all day, slow and soft rumblings, the big bass drum heartbeat giving strength to the Chief's own heartbeat. Outside, the villagers had started creating new shelters, planting sticks into the ground and weaving vines and branches around to make walls, spreading palm fronds on top as roofs, packing the earth inside firm and hard, stringing sleeping hammocks from rafters and building a cooking fire outside.

Refreshed from the river, Bella returned to the big cotton tree and helped her mother tend to Quamin, clean his ugly wound and apply a fresh layer of slimy gold juice from thick aloe cactus leaves. It did not look good. Bella could see something pale pink deep down in the wound that did not look like flesh or bone.

Quamin's fever was still high and Bella mopped his forehead, arms and legs to cool him down. Kofia spooned drops of vegetable soup in Quamin's mouth, but they dripped down his jaw as he slept and waked in and out of consciousness.

Sometimes he mumbled. One time he gave a loud shout and rose up strong from the bedding, waving an imaginary machete in his good arm, only to fall back exhausted with blood coming from his mouth and from the wound once again.

As night fell, the drums kept vigil, kept the villagers comforted, as they waited around their chief under the big cotton tree. The chants began, the songs of prayer, of hope, of Motherland, of gods and goddesses, hoping to strengthen the spirit and healing of their warrior leader.

Bella moved beside her mother and put her arm around her.

"Sleep now Mother. I will watch for a while. Put your head in my lap."

Kofia looked at her daughter. For a moment she marvelled at the woman who had grown from the small baby she birthed. A child, grown into a fighting warrior. A child who would soon be fatherless.

"I cannot sleep. He may need me." Kofia could see the depth of the wound, could see that all she could do for Quamin was to be beside him at his last breath.

"I will call you Mother. One touch and you will wake. I promise." Bella's eyes pleaded.

Kofia rested her head. Yes. It was best. Rest.

She looked at the broken body of the man who had given her a free life in this new world, this warrior of the highest nobility, a king worthy of any African kingdom, who had created his own kingdom here in the new Africa. The man who had loved her enough to give her Freedom. The man she loved. Tears finally rolled down Kofia's cheeks.

We only wanted to live free.

We have done it, Quamin and Kofia.

We lived a long life, fought many good battles.

Now the children will continue the fight to remain free.

Fight to the end. Fight to the death.

This is the death. This is the life we are fighting for.

We have to keep fighting. To be free.

To be Free! To be Free!

Finally, Kofia slept.

*   *   *   *

On the third day Kofia knew it was Quamin's last. None of her healing herbs or prayers to the spirit gods could change the fact that Quamin's wound was not healing. It went deep into his lungs and the gunpowder was rotting the soft flesh that gave him breath.

The drums were still beating. Bella rose and went outside. The entire village had gathered, waiting. She went back inside the shelter.

"Call your brothers!" Kofia's voice was urgent. "Quick! Your father wants to speak!"

Bella looked outside again and saw Johnny.

"Call my brothers! Tell them to come quick!"

Inside again, Bella saw that Quamin was now resting in Kofia's lap. Blood stained her wrap and there was blood on the bed and floor. Quamin was conscious at last, but weaker than before. He was looking up at Kofia, speaking softly to her.

"My African Queen. My beloved Empress Kofia! We have had a good life together. I shall miss you as I travel the heavens! I wish I could take you with me to visit the spirit gods!"

Kofia smiled.

"My beloved King, my African warrior! I could not have dreamed of a better life. You gave me Paradise. My heart with travel with you always. Take care of it till I see you again!"

Quamin's children gathered around him. Quamin still spoke to Kofia.

"He decrees that Kodjo will inherit as Chief" Kofia spoke Quamin's words."Give him the Chief's crown. Quako will be his lieutenant..."

"And what about me, Father? Don't leave me! Take me with you!" Bella cried out, bursting into angry tears.

Quamin whispered into Kofia's ear for a while, his chest heaving as he formed each word carefully. Then she spoke.

"Your father says he has a special duty for you to perform for him, Bella." Bella listened. "He says the warriors from the free villages in the eastern end of this new world have sent a message asking him to send someone to teach them the ways of defense he has used to keep us safe all these years. Your father wants you to go there and fulfill his promise to send someone, as he cannot now go himself."

This was an enormous honour, but an enormous responsibility for a woman. To run a village's defenses by herself would be a challenge. But Bella knew her upbringing by her father and her mother had well prepared her for this. She chose her words carefully for a moment, then spoke.

"Father, I will be happy to do whatever I can do to keep your memory alive. I will teach them the lessons I have learned as your warrior daughter. I will make you proud."

Bella saw her father's mouth make a small smile, before it returned to a look of pain from his wound. Then he whispered again in Kofia's ear and she repeated.

"Your father says he will never leave you. Whenever you call on the spirit gods, he will be there to help you fight any battle."

Bella smiled at the pleasure of that promise. "I will surely call on you Father. I will see you everywhere." She leaned forward and kissed her father's forehead.

"I love you, my Father." Tears filled Bella's eyes.

"Chief Quamin! I ask a favour as a blessing!" It was Johnny, stepping out from behind the two sons. Bella has not seem him enter with her brothers.

"The Chief says what do you ask?"

"To be allowed to go with Princess Bella to the East as her protector and helper. She should not travel so far alone."

Bella let out a gasp of surprise.

"No!" she turned to her mother, her father, her brothers. "I did not know about this! I don't need a protector...."

Kofia whispered in Quamin's ear, reminding him who Johnny was, telling him Johnny had rescued Bella's life once, had stood guard day and night as he lay ill, that he was a good warrior in battle.

Quamin whispered in Kofia's ear.

"Your father says that is a very good idea."

Johnny bowed humble, and bowed again to Bella.

She was not pleased. "Why did you ask this?" she turned to Johnny.

"I do not want to offend you Bella, only to serve you. You will need help."

Kofia spoke again. "My husband, our Chief, has made our daughter a Chieftainess, a Nanna. From now on she must be addressed with her proper title. Nanna."

Johnny bowed again. "Nanna. I am your servant."

Kodjo spoke. "It will be good for you, my sister Nanna, to have company as you travel through the land. There are many dangers on the road."

"Your sister will not be traveling on the road. Your sister will fly." Kofia spoke.

Kodjo gasped with surprise. "She will fly?"

Kofia looked proudly at Bella. "I have taught her the secret. And to Johnny also. They will be safe on that journey."

Quamin lifted his head up again and whispered in Kofia's ear. She smiled and looked deep into Quamin's face. Then she looked up at her children.

"Leave us alone now. It is time for your father and me to say our goodbye. I will sing him to sleep."

Kodjo and Quako stood and saluted Quamin. Bella could not hide her tears as she kissed the palm of Quamin's right hand – that hand that had held spear and gun so expertly in so many battles, that hand that had rocked her to sleep as a child, had pointed to hidden bird's nests on walks through the forest, had brought up shrimps from the river's deep pools.

The memories flooded Bella's mind and her tears fell on Quamin's wound that no tears could ever heal. It was hard to think this was the last time she would ever see those hands again.

Reluctantly taking a last look at their father, Bella, Kodjo, Quako and Johnny backed out of the shelter to where the drums greeted them. The pace of the drummers' fingers quickened, as they played a traveling drumbeat, the drumbeat that had called the spirit gods to their gatherings many, many times..

Kofia enveloped Quamin in her arms and began to sing a soft song, her voice twittering like a small bird, sometimes swooping like a flute, sometimes flowing like a river.

It was a song no one had ever heard before, or ever would again, for it was the song of Kofia's heart pouring out its love to her beloved Quamin, the love that would carry his spirit straight to the gods. Once securely in the home of the spirit gods, Quamin could visit her. So Kofia sang her heart, as Quamin flew on to join the spirit gods.

*   *   *   *

CHAPTER FIFTEEN

MERCY

During the first years of my service in Dr. Flint's family, I was accustomed to share some indulgences with the children of my mistress. Though this seemed to me no more than right, I was grateful for it, and tried to merit the kindness by the faithful discharge of my duties. But I now entered on my fifteenth year—a sad epoch in the life of a slave girl. My master began to whisper foul words in my ear. Young as I was, I could not remain ignorant of their import.

I tried to treat them with indifference or contempt. The master's age, my extreme youth, and the fear that his conduct would be reported to my grandmother, made him bear this treatment for many months.

He was a crafty man, and resorted to many means to accomplish his purposes. Sometimes he had stormy, terrific ways, that made his victims tremble; sometimes he assumed a gentleness that he thought must surely subdue.

Of the two, I preferred his stormy moods, although they left me trembling. He tried his utmost to corrupt the pure principles my grandmother had instilled. He peopled my young mind with unclean images, such as only a vile monster could think of. I turned from him with disgust and hatred. But he was my master. I was compelled to live under the same roof with him—where I saw a man forty years my senior daily violating the most sacred commandments of nature. He told me I was his property; that I must be subject to his will in all things. My soul revolted against the mean tyranny.

But where could I turn for protection? No matter whether the slave girl be as black as ebony or as fair as her mistress. In either case, there is no shadow of law to protect her from insult, from violence, or even from death; all these are inflicted by fiends who bear the shape of men. The mistress, who ought to protect the helpless victim, has no other feelings towards her but those of jealousy and rage. The degradation, the wrongs, the vices, that grow out of slavery, are more than I can describe. They are greater than you would willingly believe. Surely, if you credited one half the truths that are told you concerning the helpless millions suffering in this cruel bondage, you at the north would not help to tighten the yoke. You surely would refuse to do for the master, on your own soil, the mean and cruel work which trained bloodhounds and the lowest class of whites do for him at the south.

Everywhere the years bring to all enough of sin and sorrow; but in slavery the very dawn of life is darkened by these shadows. Even the little child, who is accustomed to wait on her mistress and her children, will learn, before she is twelve years old, why it is that her mistress hates such and such a one among the slaves. Perhaps the child's own mother is among those hated ones. She listens to violent outbreaks of jealous passion, and cannot help understanding what is the cause. She will become prematurely knowing in evil things. Soon she will learn to tremble when she hears her master's footfall. She will be compelled to realize that she is no longer a child.

If God has bestowed beauty upon her, it will prove her greatest curse. That which commands admiration in the white woman only hastens the degradation of the female slave. I know that some are too much brutalized by slavery to feel the humiliation of their position; but many slaves feel it most acutely, and shrink from the memory of it. I cannot tell how much I suffered in the presence of these wrongs, nor how I am still pained by the retrospect.

My master met me at every turn, reminding me that I belonged to him, and swearing by heaven and earth that he would compel me to submit to him. If I went out for a breath of fresh air, after a day of unwearied toil, his footsteps dogged me. If I knelt by my mother's grave, his dark shadow fell on me even there. The light heart which nature had given me became heavy with sad forebodings. The other slaves in my master's house noticed the change. Many of them pitied me; but none dared to ask the cause. They had no need to inquire. They knew too well the guilty practices under that roof; and they were aware that to speak of them was an offence that never went unpunished.

I longed for some one to confide in. I would have given the world to have laid my head on my grandmother's faithful bosom, and told her all my troubles. But Dr. Flint swore he would kill me, if I was not as silent as the grave. [6]

*   *   *

---

[6]"From Incidents in the Life of a Slave Girl,"
Microsoft® Encarta® Africana 2000. © 1999 Microsoft
Corporation. All rights reserved.

FALMOUTH, JAMAICA

1764

The clip clop of the horses hooves clattered incessantly in Mercy's ears. She pulled the shawl around her ears and huddled in her jacket from the wind that rushed past them, and wished that she could be riding inside the carriage beside her mistress, the lady Anne Ratcliffe.

The journey from the estate in Portland to Falmouth had started at daybreak, when the sun was cool, then continued into the heat of middle day from which Mercy barely sheltered under her thin straw hat. Now night had come and she was looking forward to the expected overnight stop at the inn at White River.

Beside Mercy sat the driver. He had not spoken to her all day, hardly glanced sideways at her as he guided the animals along the rutted roads. Now that it was night, Mercy was glad he was silent, as with his dark skin and clothing, he was almost invisible and she could imagine herself rushing alone into the dark behind mysterious steeds hurtling to a destination far more interesting than the night that actually lay ahead of her.

Mercy knew that on arrival at the inn, while Miss Ratcliffe would be immediately be swept upstairs to the best room, her first task would be to find the well and start drawing water for Miss Ratcliffe's bath, lifting the heavy buckets up the stone stairs and emptying them into the tub in Miss Ratcliffe's room. She knew Miss Ratcliffe would be waiting each time she emptied the bucket, feigning inability to remove her clothes, so Mercy would be down on her knees unbuttoning boots, removing stockings, then unlacing corset, unpinning hair, brushing hair, unpacking the bag containing her sleepwear and placing the silk garments on the bed.

Finally, when enough buckets of water had been brought and Miss Ratcliffe finally undressed, Mercy would soap the sponge and bathe Miss Ratcliffe. Then, tired as she then was, her duty was to fetch Miss Ratcliffe's dinner from the kitchen on a tray, wait outside the door until she had finished and return the tray and dishes.

Only then could Mercy venture to the slave hut in search of food and a rest place for herself. Sleep was elusive in the strange barracks of snoring women, and dawn was a good excuse to rise up and start preparing for Miss Ratcliffe's departure.

As she emerged from the slave hut, she found herself staring into the face of the buggy driver. His eyes hardened, his lips curled and, turning his head slightly, he spat on the ground. Then he moved aside.

Mercy hurried to the river. She was by now accustomed to the looks of hatred she received from many of her fellow slaves. As she bent over to step into the water, she caught a glimpse of her reflection. She could see her pale skin and the honey blonde curls that fell over her shoulder. She couldn't see her eyes, but she knew – for others had told her – that they were green. Mercy knew she looked almost as 'white' as her European owner, Miss Ratcliffe.

Only a slight thickening of her nostrils imprinted her African genes. These Mercy inherited from her African mother Amina, herself powerless to avoid the rape and lifelong role as bed slave of her English owner, Mercy's father. So how could Mercy be blamed for her colour, when it did not excuse her from the same treatment others darker-skinned than she endued. She was still a 'nigger' slave.

Mercy sat by the river and wished she had someone to tell her life to, someone who could help explain why it all seemed so unfair, full of hatred, pain and suffering. She wished her mother was still close, she wanted to feel her mother's strong arms around her, she wanted to hear her mother's voice in her ears telling her not to be discouraged with the sorrow and pain of her live, but to be strong, invincible and ultimately victorious in the battle of life and death that had been Mercy's life this far.

But her mother Pibba was no longer close to comfort her. Pibba had been sold four years ago when she started complaining about Massa Ratcliffe's assaults on Mercy's body.

"You must not do that Massa," she could hear her mother's voice pleading, holding tightly to her 14 year-old daughter's body, as Massa Ratcliffe dragged Mercy by the hand out of the slave barracks towards the GreatHouse.

"She is too young! She is your own child! This is WRONG!!!" Mercy could hear her mother Pibba's angry shouts and see the flood of tears that washed her face. But her mother's tears could not stop Massa Ratcliffe. He could do whatever he wanted with his slaves, and he wanted Mercy.

"Shush, Mama!" Mercy begged her. "I don't want you to get another lashing. Let me go. I will do what he wants.

Just stop talking. Wait here for me; I will soon come back. Please Mama!"

Mercy had gritted her teeth together to endure the pain she knew she would suffer from Massa Ratclife's hands and body, but she knew her mother would be there when she returned, to comfort her and put soft poultices on her private places.

But not for long. Massa Ratcliffe decided that if lashings could not silence Pibba, then he would remove her to where she could no longer interfere with his pleasure.

Mercy remembered the heartbreak of the day her mother Pibba was taken from the plantation to be sold. She shook from her mind the memory of her pitiful cries, her mother's pleading to Massa Ratcliffe:

"I beg you Massa! Don't sell me! Don't' take me from my daughter! I will do whatever you want! Extra work! Hard work! DON'T SELL ME MASSA, I BEG YOU!!!"

But Massa Ratcliffe sat on the Great House verandah with a sneer on his face, sipping a glass of rum, pretending not to hear the heartbreaking voices.

She shook from her memory the crowd of women standing, watching, silent as they had to be or risk a beating or even the same fate as Pibba, who enveloped her in their arms and held her back as she stretched out her hands to try and reach her mother who was now out of her reach, who hugged her to their bosoms and held her tight as she shook with sobs, bawling out to her mother:

"Mama! Mama! Don't leave me! MAMA! MAMA! MAMA!"

The wheels of the cart and the steps of the donkey that hauled it crunched on the stony road. Mercy could see Pibba' face through the slats in the side of the cart. She could hear her mother's voice calling her name.

"MERCY! MERCY! MERCY!"

They held Mercy, for she was too weak to stand. They held her as she watched the cart disappear down the road, further and further away from her, until finally, sadly, the last glimpse of her mother disappeared.

They held her through the night, as her tears boiled hot from the fever that gripped her body, crying, crying, crying. How could she continue to live without her beloved mother? They offered themselves as replacement, knowing full well they could never replace a mother's love, the strength of which not even slavery could diminish

Now at 18, Mercy was exhausted by the bitterness of life. Her tears splashed into the river's flow, vanishing as her mother had done on that sad day. But life had also taught Mercy that tears are a forbidden luxury for a slave. She splashed the cool river water over her face, wet her long golden brown hair and smoothed it into a thick bun at her neck, tied her head, pulled on her dress and she set her feet in her slippers.

Miss Ratcliffe would be up and waiting for her. Hardly dried off from her river bath, Mercy rushed back to the Inn and up the stairs of the servants entrance, running breathlessly down the wood-floored passage to Miss Ratcliffe's room. Her mistress was fortunately still in bed, but yawned, got out of bed and – surprisingly – began to dress herself.

"I am sorry I took so long," Mercy hurried to help her mistress. But Miss Ratcliffe pushed her rudely aside.

"I shall have to get used to doing for myself now," she snapped.

Mercy hardly understood. "What do you mean, Mistress? Am I not doing a good job any more?"

Miss Ratcliffe paused and turned her head over her shoulder, smiling wickedly.

"You are soon going to be out of my sight forever. Out of MY sight and out of my husband's eyes, you shameless coquette. I've sold you!

"Sold me! Oh no Mistress! Please don't send me to another plantation! Don't separate me from the only family I know!" She flung herself to the floor, grasping at Miss Ratcliffe's ankles. Miss Ratcliffe freed herself with a kick that landed in Mercy's stomach.

"Get away from me! I don't want you to touch me ever again! Today I am free of you at last! Get dressed. Put on your best clothes and make sure you're clean."

Mercy crawled into a corner of the room, sobbing loudly. Another swift kick from Miss Ratcliffe and her sobs quieted into wet gulping breaths. Now she understood the purpose of this journey. She wondered which plantation she had been sold to and hoped it was close to Egypt, so she could visit her mother and her sisters and brothers. A stab of pain stuck her heart, as she realized she might never see her mother again. How could she find out where her mother was, which plantation she had been sold to, if she herself was to be sold!

Mercy's mind flashed with a memory of the lessons her mother taught her on nights when the full moon was bright. On those nights Pibba would tell Mercy the stories of her ancestors, of their brave fights against the slave masters, of how they called on the ancient African spirits to make their minds strong and their hearts brave, of how to make healing medicines from the plants and animals, of how to transform themselves into birds, trees, stones. The 'Moon Secrets" Mercy called those lessons.

"Oh God," Mercy prayed. "Let me see my mother one more time again. Let me hear her voice, let me hug her and receive her hug one more time, Let me feel her hand stroking my forehead, telling me that everything bad will be alright, bringing me stolen food hidden in the folds of her apron, shushing me after the pain of sex with the Massa, telling me to endure and be strong .... Oh God, just let me just see my mother one more time!" she prayed.

Mercy's prayer was not to be answered.

*   *   *   *

Falmouth was a shock for Mercy. The notorious town where slaves were unloaded and sold was a place where men exercised their worst animal behaviours. Sailors, released from their bondage on savage ships, sought women and wenches to wipe some of the worst memories and strengthen them for more on future voyages. After the merciless voyages across the African Ocean, the town of Falmouth was like all the other slave ports on the island and in the other islands of the Caribbean archipelago.

Perched on the edge of a harbour in which rested several sailing ships, the sea lapped at the town's feet, a stinking hellhole of the island polluted by the crimes of the people who inhabited it and made money in it, much more than the smell of fish caught by small fishing boats at rest in the harbour.

Well-dressed men and women, sailors in ragged clothes, women in fine dresses and wenches in less, filled the streets. The bars and whorehouses that lined the cobbled walkways rang day and night with the sounds of debauchery, loud laughter, drinking, singing and wild music, while the business of commerce in slaves and goods being conducted at all times lent an even more greedy tone to the town's devilish activities.

It was to one of the whorehouses that Mercy was taken, a set of rooms above one of the larger bars in the town's main street. The woman to whom she was sold prided herself on offering girls that closely resembled white Europeans through mixed-race origins similar to Mercy's. Some of her 'girls' had gratefully accepted this job as an easier work than the plantation, but there were many like Mercy who had been dumped there because of how closely they resembled a guilty plantation owner.

The transaction complete, Mrs. Ratcliffe placed the bag of coins Mercy had been sold for into her purse, gave her one last scornful look and swept downstairs back to her carriage and away from Falmouth. Mercy was thrown like a bundle of clothing in a corner of a small windowless cubicle at one end of a dark corridor and her bag of small possessions thrown in behind her. Mercy buried her face in her hands and wept until the river of her tears had washed her emotions dry. Then she faced her fears.

Where was she? What was this place? What were her duties?

She soon found answers.

As night of Mercy's first day was falling, the door of her cubicle opened and the woman whose husband had bought Mercy entered.

"I am Mrs. Esmie Brottan. Miss Esmie to you!" She spoke loudly with a menacing stare. Pushing a bowL of cold porridge to Mercy, she ordered: "Eat, then clean up yourself. The night is just beginning."

She weht out the door and locked it behind her.

Mercy ate the porridge, then straightened her clothes to wait for whatever duties she would be asked to perform. She reminded herself of the housekeeping work she had done on the Ratcliffe plantation and knew that whatever job she was assigned to, she would do it well.

What a surprise awaited Mercy!

The door was unlocked and inside fell a huge white man, fully dressed including his three-corner hat and a bottle of rum in his hand that splashed over Mercy as he fell so the floor. Pinning Mercy to the thin carpet that covered part of the room, he used her body exactly as Massa Ratcliffe had done.

Shocked, but not unaccustomed to the actions of drunk white men, Mercy gathered her clothes around her when he was finished and waited for Miss Esmie to arrive, explain and apologize for the liberty that had been taken with her slave and assign her duties. But to her greater shock, the room soon opened again and another almost identical white man came in and did the same as the first.

It was only when the assaults ended 7 men later, that Mercy realized where she was and what her duties were.

In the sunlight hours that were hers the next day, Mercy forced her mind back to the lessons her mother had taught her on full moon nights. "The Secrets of the Moon Time" was how her mother would describe the words of wisdom she shared with her daughter.

"The Moon Time Secrets were brought from Africa with Kofia, your great, great grandmother," Pibba would tell Mercy when she was still a child, but old enough to start learning the lessons.

"Your Ancestor Kofia was a great woman who brought the warrior spirit with her from Africa and placed it like a seed in all the women she gave birth to in the New Country," she explained. "She gave birth to two sons and a daughter Bella. She became the great warrior chieftainess Nanna, who led the Eastern free Africans and made a nation of Free Africans in the high mountains where the big river flows they call the Grande. Nanna used the Moon Secrets to fight against the slavemasters, to keep the Eastern Africans safe and free. She ruled over the eastern mountains and their valleys and if there had been more warriors like her, all of us Africans would be living free today, making life for ourselves."

"I have heard stories about Nanna when I was a child," Mercy nodded. "Sometimes I would hear the older slaves talk about Nanna, the African warrior woman who led the free people who lived in the mountains and could not be defeated in battle, but I thought these were just stories. I didn't know Nanna was a real person!"

"She was my grandmother?"

"Yes," Pibba confirmed. "She was MY mother and she was truly great. Everything they say about her is true. She was a wise woman, a priestess too, she could call on the

Spirit Gods to help her win battles. She would call out to her father, King Quamin, to help her win the battle!"

"What!" Mercy was astonished. "And he would hear her?

Pibba smiled. "It seems so. She was always victorious. She used to chant as she fought, shouting out words we didn't understand, words from the Spirit Gods. Her people worshipped her, both as a warrior and as a woman. They saw her as their mother, taking care of them as if they were all her children. She was such a good ruler the people named the village they lived in after her, Nanna Town."

There was silence, as Mercy absorbed the information and created a vision in her mind of her ancestor.

"Where is she now?" Mercy had heard about the Maroons.

"The Western Maroons signed a Treaty with the Governor that gave them freedom if they would stop fighting the rulers and the system of plantation slavery, Pibba explained. "Queen Mother Nanna did not agree to sign that Treaty, she said we should keep fighting till every slave was free. So they fought her and fought her and fought her until they conquered Nanna Town."

"But if your mother – my grandmother – was free, why are you and I slaves now?"   "There was one battle she did not win." Pibba looked away, trying to obscure the memory.

"This time when the soldiers captured Nanna Town, they took all the women and children they found there. Nanna would not let them capture her. Rather than fall into their hands, she jumped off a cliff."

"What?" Mercy was shocked. "She gave up her life like that?"

"Some tales say she did not jump,"

Pibba spoke quietly.

"Some say she flew away, the same way she came from the West of the island to live with us in the East. They say she flew away back to Africa."

"She flew? People can't fly!" Mercy was astonished.

"Oh yes, my child," she nodded her chin. "In those times, the people could fly like birds. Nanna flew to the East as a white owl, the night she flew to the East to lead the people's fight for freedom. That is why they accepted her, a woman, as their leader. Only special people know how to fly."

"So why didn't you fly away with your mother?" Mercy wanted to know.

"She had not taught me that Secret yet. I was only a child, too young to learn. Now the knowledge has been lost when Nanna flew away."

"So how did you come to this plantation?"

"After the battle, the soldiers took me and anyone who was still alive when they reached on our village. Pibba did not like remembering. "It was mostly children, as those who could not escape, killed themselves so they would die as free people. My sister Amina and I were two of the children they took. We are children of Nanna. "

Mercy was listening, learning her history.

"Queen Nanna knew a lot of the scientific knowledge that makes the earth turn and the sun rise and set. She knew about nature also, and how nature and science work together. Her mother, and her mother's mother before, and all the people of our country, knew that there was special knowledge that kept us alive and healthy in time of plenty and of loss, and that it was important to keep all that knowledge in our people, inside our brains, from parent to child, generation to generation, forever.

"When they took us from Africa, they took everything when they took our bodies, but they could not take the knowledge that was in our brains and our spirit. They could not take away our ways of speaking to our Spirit Gods, of healing our sick, of creating new expressions of our culture. These are some of the Secrets, the knowledge that has kept us alive through the times and places we have been living in, and we must keep that knowledge safe to keep us safe."

"Your grandmother Nanna taught me the Moon Secrets and I am teaching them to you so you can teach your own children when you have them."

"I don't plan to have any children," Mercy was defiant. "I don't see any man I want to be with."

Pibba smiled. "You are only 12 years old now. But one day a man will choose you. As a slave you have no choice. You will either accept him or despise him. Pray for one you can accept, then your life will be less miserable"

Mercy considered this, then spoke.

"So teach me Mama, what to do with a man to make life better."

"Your body is a powerful weapon," said her mother softly, "and if you use it to entice a man that you want, he will become your slave. This may seem good, but when you are tired of him, he will become angry and hate you. That is the worst enemy to have – a former lover who hates you. Let your body be a gift of love to a man that he will treasure like precious jewels, then he will give you love for ever."

Mercy considered this quietly.

"Only use your body to entice if your life is in danger. Then this is what you must do."

Mercy's mother spoke softly into her ear, then folded the flap over as if to seal in the knowledge. In that small cubicle of a Falmouth whorehouse, Mercy remembered that lesson well and her mother's words repeated in her head. She rested and thought out her plan.

That night, Mercy endured the assaulting line of men, gritting her teeth at each entry as if she was in another place and time. She was waiting, and she knew her wait would be rewarded.

She was right.

He was back.

The man who had said: "You're too beautiful for this place."

As he stepped in, Mercy recognized him.

Before he could fall on her, Mercy stretched out her hand to him and looked him in the eye with a small smile. Then with the other hand she slowly unrolled her hair from the tight bun at the back of her neck in which she kept her beautiful shower of long golden curls, the beautiful hair that marked her so clearly as Mr. Ratcliffe's offspring even more than her pale skin and slender nose. As the golden silk tumbled over her shoulders towards her waist, Mercy pulled her shift off her shoulders and down over her golden body.

The she watched as the shock at the sight of her beauty brought him to orgasm without even touching her.

*   *   *

The cabin of a ship's captain was a far more comfortable abode than Miss Esmie's cubicle, and certainly than the slave barracks of the Ratcliffe plantation.

Rolling up her beautiful curls into a manageable bun at her neck, Mercy reached inside her bag of possessions and amid the few pieces of clothing, pulled out a small book, opened it and placed her finger on the first word. Now she would have time and opportunity to continue learning the words she heard Mrs. Ratcliffe teaching her daughter out of this same little book, the precious thing she had taken with her on the journey to Kingston that fateful night.

Tossing the bag and the rest of its contents out the open porthole, Mercy said goodbye to her former life, lay back on the captain's bed and thanked God silently for her rescue.

Sea-sickness on the journey to England, and satisfying the drunken Captain Grant's constant sexual demands, were a minor price to pay for the life that awaited Mercy as the freed wench of a rich ship's captain and soon-to-be English Lord and landowner.

CHAPTER SIXTEEN

ELISABETH

LONDON 1973

Elisabeth pushed her suitcase out the door, slammed it and turned the key, then with boots under one arm and her gown in the zipped-up bag over her other arm, dragged everything down the single flight of stairs outside her flat to the heavy entrance door, outside which she could hear Mark tooting his horn impatiently.

She opened the door to a sunny London afternoon, the joys of summer obvious in the open windows of the elegant flats lining the streets of her Knightsbridge neighbourhood, the scenes of leisure in the tree-lined park they surrounded, and the casual-elegant clothes of passersby.

"Give a hand!" she shouted to him. Mark climbed out of the Rover, helped her down the steps to the sidewalk, opened the trunk and put the suitcase and boots inside, while Elizabeth opened the rear door and laid her gown bag neatly on the seat.

"For heaven's sake, Elisabeth." Mark's impatience showed. "It's just a weekend party, you're not moving house!"

Elisabeth just smiled. She was getting used to Mark's easy anger. She had the remedy to cool it. She waited till he re-entered the car and turned on the ignition. Making sure her already-short skirt was revealing lots of her smooth inner thigh, she reached her arm around his shoulder and leaned forward to give him a kiss on the cheek, knowing that the swell of her breasts were even more visible with that gesture.

Yes, the anger disappeared. Instead, a slight swell rose in his lap. Elisabeth reached her other hand to the swelling, but Mark quickly brushed it away.

"Come on, let's go. We want to be there before night," was all he could say, putting the car into gear and moving off from the Sloane Street sidewalk.

"I know it seems like a lot of luggage, Elisabeth pouted slightly, "but I want to make sure I have enough choices, just in case."

"Just in case of what? It's not Royal wedding happening this weekend, you know." Mark was still annoyed.

Elisabeth smiled. "It's not every day I get to meet my future in-laws. How I look is as important as how I behave, and I am going to give them no chance to fault me on either."

*   *   *   *

Elisabeth turned on the radio, tuned it to the pirate radio station broadcasting pop music from outside England's territorial waters, pushed her blonde hair out of her face and leaned back on the car's soft leather upholstery whose smell confirmed the wealth of the man she sat beside. There was time to think, as she watched the London cityscape melt away into one motorway then another, then branch off through the farms and forests into the country roads of Buckinghamshire and then Dorset towards Ashford Manor.

She was apprehensive about the weekend. She had already met Mark's older brother Stephen early on in her seven-month relationship with Mark, and she found him as charming as his brother. Mark had even introduced her to his mother, at least on the telephone when she had called Mark's flat one Sunday morning when Elisabeth had slept overnight.

"Mama, say Hello to Elisabeth," he had said and handed the phone across the bed to her. Shocked, but composed, Elisabeth said "Good Morning Lady Ashford," then hadn't known what to say next. She couldn't exactly say "Pleased to meet you," over the phone. She was sure she could hear in the silence that followed that Lady Ashsford did not approve of the 'free love' habits of the new generation of women liberated by the Pill, the women's movement and hippies.

So instead, she had simply said "Looking forward to meeting you," as brightly as she could and handed the phone back to Mark.

Now she was going to meet Lord and Lady Ashford, hereditary peers and lords of Ashford Manor stately home, open to the public for 3 months a year, but retained as a family residence for the past 300 years. Well at least our families are equal, Elisabeth smiled at the comforting fact that her aristocratic lineage was as noble and even older than theirs.

She was the eldest daughter of Viscount Falmouth, a peerage was bestowed in 1776 on his ancestor Captain James Grant by a grateful sovereign in reward for services in the British Navy. The Ashford's title was even newer than her father's, and only a baronetcy not a peerage, so social equality - if not supremacy -- had already been established.

Elisabeth knew her parents would be happy if she married Mark. Union of two aristocratic families whose fortunes were still intact, was the dream of every titled parent. Mark was the man they had always dreamed she would marry, wealthy, handsome and adventurous, like she was. They had met while she was on her family's annual ski trip to Gstaad; he was with a group of four of his friends from Cambridge where he was reading History. Back home in London, they partied at Annabels, dined at the 'Trat' and enjoyed the best seats at pop music concerts by Hendrix, the Stones and Tom Jones.

Elisabeth's trust fund meant her job as sometime receptionist for her friend Suzanne's Kings Road boutique was just an opportunity to get first choice of the most fashionable clothes, and Suzanne was always forgiving of late arrivals or even no-shows, after the occasional Great Night Out or Long Weekend at Mark's Belgrave Square apartment.

Now this long weekend would be devoted to the special joys of a grand country wedding party, as Mark served as best man for his brother Stephen's walk down the aisle with his Danish fiancee. Elisabeth smiled with anticipation of the good time to come.

It was nearly dark as the Rover turned into the private road leading through the Ashford estate, and after winding through a forest of beech trees, flat farms of barley on either side, past a lake, then stables and barns, the car drove through high iron gates of the entrance of Ashsford Manor. Gardeners were putting finishing touches to the lawn, landscapers were packing pots of flowers into the decorative gardens surrounding the fountain, while at one end of the lawn two huge tents were swallowing up an endless flow of tables, chairs and tablecloths in anticipation of tomorrow's ceremony.

A uniformed butler stepped down from the massive oak entrance doors and opened the door on Elisabeth's side of the car, while Mark came around from his side, handing his keys to the butler.

"Luggage in the trunk, Simpson. You will know which room."

Elisabeth turned to open the back door and take her gown, but Mark held her back. "Simpson will do it. Come let's go meet Mama."

The long hallway was lined with paintings of former family members, reminding Elisabeth of her own home's decor, huge portraits of men, women and children in period clothes and serious faces. Mark led her into the drawing room, a large high-ceilinged space filled with gilded Louis IV chairs and sofas upholstered in wine velvet and flower-patterned drapes covering French windows, opening onto a conservatory at the far end filled with ferns, orchids and vases of peonies.

Gentlemen stood by a large table in one corner that held bottles of drinks of all kinds and several sizes of glasses. Women and men moved with ease around the room, drinking, smoking and talking with each other. Mark strode in, towards a slight woman seated in a high-backed, gilded chair like a queen on her throne.

"MaMAH!" he shouted, emphasis on the second syllable. The two embraced tightly.

"You naughty boy!" she chided in mock complaint. "Takes a wedding to get you to come and visit your Mother," she smiled. Then, as if just realizing that there was someone else with Mark, she turned to acknowledge Elisabeth, stretching out her hand. "This must be Elisabeth! Come, let me see you!"

The hand Lady Ashford stretched out to Elisabeth was adorned with jewels. Around her wrist were three gold and diamond bracelets. On each finger were lumps of coloured gems secured into cages of gold, silver and platinum, keeping each other company in a sparkling display of wealth.

Afraid to trap the soft flesh of her right hand in such metallic danger, Elisabeth used her left hand to grasp the ends of flesh offered and sank down in a small curtsey in front of her. Lady Ashford smiled at the unnecessary, but welcome, gesture.

"Ah Elisabeth! Pretty girl! Come sit here beside me," she said, indicating a velvet-covered hassock nearby. "Mark you always had a good eye for picking women," she twinkled at Mark, who raised his eyes to heaven in a look of desperation, murmuring "MaMA ..."

Ignoring Mark, Lady Ashford turned to Elisabeth. "Welcome to Ashford Manor. I hope you will enjoy your stay. I can't imagine why a lovely girl like you should have allowed yourself to be enticed by a reprobate like my son Mark. Stephen is a much better choice of husband, but then the Danish girl has already bagged him, hasn't she! Ha Ha Ha!"

Elisabeth looked around her at the others in the room, but they had already turned back to their conversations as if they were very accustomed to Lady's Ashford's outrgeousness.

"Mark is just my good friend, Lady Ashford," she smiled and hoped she sounded believable.

Lady Ashford leaned forward to Elisabeth, her necklace of amethysts with a teardrop pear pendant glistening as it flopped over her chest, to whisper a little too loudly in her ear:

"Always best to stay friends, dear girl. I hear the Pill is very effective protection nowadays. Do you find it so?"

Elisabeth could not cover her shock quickly. 'No! ... I mean Yes ... I mean..."

Elisabeth used a diaphragm herself -- convenient, with no danger of after-effects -- but she could not discuss her contraceptive methods with this strange, very strange woman, even if she was her boyfriend's mother. She looked around desperately to find Mark, who was on his way back from the drinks table with a glass of champagne for Elisabeth and a glass of something else for his mother.

"Hope you mixed it right, Mark dear." His mother stretched out her hand for it. Sipping it, she remarked "Too much gin, not enough vermouth, but not bad for the first of the weekend. Little stronger next time," she said.

Elisabeth took the opportunity to rise from the hassock and take the champagne flute from Mark, slipping her arm into his and gently steering him towards the conservatory. "Show me the orchids, please." Then as they reached the relative privacy behind a huge vase of flowers, she collapsed on Mark's shoulder.

"Your mother ....." Elisabeth couldn't continue.

"Oh ... Mama's started already." A slight frown passed his face. "Guess she's been drinking ever since they laid out the drinks table. Did she say something to upset you? Never mind; no one takes anything Mama says seriously these days. I just love her and leave her," he smiled.

"I feel a little tired. Can we find our room now," Elisabeth pleaded.

"Not our room this weekend. Mama would never allow us to be sleeping together. You're in my room and I am bunking in the single men's tent. It's that one in the rear courtyard. They know we're all going to make a lot of noise when we get drunk later after everyone's gone to bed, so they farm us out back there and we all have a grand time. Come," he took Elisabeth's hand. "I'll show you the way to my room. There's a secret passage behind the stairs."

Elisabeth stretched out on the huge bed that stood high off the floor, covered in a thick down-filled duvet. It was definitely a man's room, hockey sticks and football boots in the corners, posters of football players and beautiful women on one wall and a large painting of a 17th Century hunting scene hung over the fireplace. Her suitcase had been unpacked, her toilet articles placed neatly in the bathroom and her gown unzipped from its plastic case, now hung neatly from a hanger on the huge armoire.

So this was her family-to-be. Elisabeth thought about all that had happened so far and how meeting Mark's mother had made her realize how little she knew about him and his family. She took the rest she knew she would need later, for she knew well what the weekend held and what awaited her tonight, as the family and friends close enough to be housed in the massive mansion gathered for the wedding. As a member of Britain's wealthy aristocratic families, she had attended enough similar parties from nursery days, through high school, debutante year and now as a young woman.

She knew and anticipated with dread the endless polite conversations at drinks before dinner, the mindless chatter through all five courses at dinner served by white-gloved servants, the absolutely boring conversations that came with the after-dinner coffee, brandy, port, whisky, wine and liqueurs ... conversations about family and times past and children and school and, eventually, politics, the government and the world.

Some guests would become drunk, some obnoxious, some rude, some foolish, but everything -- whether insane or profane -- would be politely forgiven, laughed off and forgotten the next day.

Reluctantly Elisabeth roused from the bed. She took a bath, then changed into a black cocktail dress, draped her pearls around her neck, slipped into silver high-heeled sandals that matched her silver clutch purse and steeled herself for the night ahead. With no way to contact Mark, she decided to find her way downstairs herself. She opened the door and looked right and left, wondering which was the way to go. The corridor stretched equally on both sides and she had no idea which was the door that opened to the secret passageway through which Mark had brought her to the room.

Hearing voices from a room far away on the right, she decided to knock there and ask the way, but as soon as she came to the door she realized that the voice she heard was Mark's mother conversing with someone else. Determined not to have another encounter so soon with Lady Ashford, she saw there was another passage on the left, so she turned there and soon found a staircase that led towards light and the sound of a piano being played.

The staircase was carpeted with red velvet with baroque gold uprights that stretched down into the living room, in which the weekend guests relaxed with drinks and chatter over the tinkle of music. Elisabeth stopped with a shock as she saw the descent she had to make, but then took a deep breath and, making sure to be sure-footed and not fall, came down one step at a time, making an entrance worthy of a princess that caught the admiration of all the men present, and the envy of a few women.

Mark rushed to her side. "I was just coming to get you. Everyone's waiting for Mama. She's still upstairs." Taking her arm, he proudly escorted Elisabeth around the room, introducing her to relatives and friends and pausing long enough with each to bring everyone into a party spirit.

His brother Stephen and his bride-to-be Lady Annella Fenwood were seated specially in the grandest corner of the room. Mark steered Elisabeth towards them and she was glad to join in the warmth of the congratulations they were receiving. Ailsa, Stephen's fiancee slipped her arm into Elisabeth's. "Good to see you! Tomorrow I'll show you the presents!"

Mark's father had not yet arrived at the Manor, but Mark explained that Lord Ashford would be driven over by his chaffeur later that night from his job 'in the City' that kept him busy too often to spend many weekends at Ashford.

Soon Lady Ashford descended down the staircase, sweeping the train of her evening gown over one arm while holding on to the steadying arm of another woman. The woman was short and dressed simply in dark clothes and a shawl draped over her head. She held her head down and did not look at any of the guests, not as if she was shy but as if she was unaware of their presence or did not care.

""Oh no, not that woman again," she heard Mark whisper under his breath as he took her arm to join the procession into the dining room. "I don't know why Mama invited her this weekend."

"Who is she?"

Mark sighed. "I guess you could call her Mama's guru. She reads tea leaves and tells fortunes. Mama met her at a country fair and became entranced with her prophecies. I suppose she's here to entertain the guests, but she has a peculiar spirit that I don't particularly like, especially not how mesmerized Mama is by her."

The butler announced: "Dinner is served." The procession into the dining room was led by Lady Ashford, the short woman padding silently beside her with bowed head, looking like an oversized shaggy dog.

The seating arrangements placed Stephen and Ailsa on her left and Mark and Elisabeth on her right, with guests arranged down the length of the 20-seater grand dining table and an empty chair at the other end awaiting Lord Ashford's arrival. Unusually, the strange woman did not occupy a seat at the table, but sat on a low stool placed slightly behind Lady's Ashford right side.

A wedding-eve dinner was a very special affair, with course after course of gourmet food served by a team of uniformed, white-gloved servants, vintage wines with each course to accompany the many toasts to the health and happiness of the bride and groom, some family jokes and even a saucy story or two as the wine took effect on those who drank their fill.

As dinner proceeded Lady Ashford placed small forkfulls of her own food into a small silver bowl the woman cupped in her hands. She drank neither wine nor water and placed the food in her mouth with her hands, head bowed so the shawl draped over her head fell shaded her face and actions.

When she raised her head, she seemed to fix Elisabeth with a deep stare that was startling in the amount of hatred it conveyed. Elisabeth tried not to look or pay much attention to the woman, but instead looked the other way, smiled and made cross-table conversation with Ailsa about the wedding, honeymoon plans, and even made brief polite conversation with the elderly gentleman on her other side for long enough to find out that he was the Ashford family banker.

But every time she turned to back to the comfort of Mark's smile and small talk, she was confronted with the woman's stare, a hot fire that seared into her consciousness. It puzzled her. What could be the matter with this strange woman, she wondered, as the woman's presence was taking all the joy out of the anticipated pleasure the weekend had promised.

Coffee was served and servants placed dainty silver pedestals at intervals along the table offering tasty gourmet chocolates, dipped strawberries, cashew brittle and macaroons.

That's when the woman spoke for the first time. Her voice was like sandpaper on gravel.

"You want to marry Mark."

It was not a question, but a statement.

Elisabeth was shocked, confused, didn't know how to answer. She decided to answer simply.

"Yes, Mark and I are going to be married."

"You WANT to marry Mark, but it will not happen."

The volume of the woman's voice was like a bullhorn, cutting the dinner table conversation instantly silent, and fixing the attention of everyone present on her now unshaded face.

The woman fixed her eyes into the depth of Elisabeth's own.

"You are the eldest daughter of Viscount Falmouth, descendant of Captain James Grant, a British sailor given his peerage in 1759 as thanks from a grateful King for the many treasures he brought from the Spanish and French ships of the Caribbean seas."

"Yes," Elisabeth ventured a small smile, surprised that what sounded like praise of the history of her ancestor should be voiced with so much anger. Her smile froze at the woman's next words.

"The most favourite treasure Captain Grant brought from the Caribbean was his Jamaican wife ... *a nigger slave!*" she shouted.

*   *   *   *

They had been driving in silence for the past two hours through the dark countryside roads and then the motorway, as now as the car entered the narrow streets of

London's Knightsbridge townhouses, Elisabeth felt it was best for her to be the first to speak.

The nightmare of leaving the table, hurriedly pushing her clothes back into her travel bag (the hell with the wedding party frock), pushing back the tears that flowed down her face as she dragged the suitcase down the hallway, ignoring the guests loitering with wine glasses in hands as they watched her rush past their gossiping conversations about her that silenced as she passed.

Leaving the house, walking down the long driveway dragging her bag behind her towards the high iron gates, wondering how she would open them, until the lights and sound of a car behind her brought Mark to a stop beside her and, without a word being spoken, she and her suitcase were pushed into the car, the estate gates opened by remote control and the two-hour drive back to London began.

The silence of words in the car was a contrast to the noise in Elisabeth's head. Over and over she heard the words spew from that awful woman's mouth. Over and over! *"A nigger slave! A nigger slave! A NIGGER SLAVE!"*

Worse were the words she followed with: "No black babies for the Ashfords, thank you."

Elisabeth had jumped to her feet and pushed over her chair.

"Oh my God! What are you saying! Are you CRAZY?"

Everything seemed frozen in time, colour was drained from the scene and everything she was seeing appeared in shades of black and gray and white.

She thought she would faint, but then she told herself not to give the old witch the pleasure of seeing the hurt her words had caused. She would remove herself instead with dignity. She saw the frowns of shock and disapproval on everyone's faces as she rushed from the table, hurling at the woman the only curse she could think of that didn't include swearwords:

"You evil witch! May God punish you!!!"

*   *   *   *

Packing and leaving had been a blur, Elisabeth was sure she had forgotten something. She could only think of one thing: What did she mean? What did she mean?

Elisabeth was so shocked, her heart was pounding in rhythm to the noise in her head. She leaned back and let Mark drive. Then she turned her head to the window and wept. Whatever that woman said, it had broken her relationship with Mark. Nothing would ever be the same, after the shame of her embarrassment in front of his closest family and friends. She didn't care what Mark's family thought of her now, but she cared about what Mark thought.

The Rover purred to a stop outside Elisabeth's building and Mark turned off the engine.

"It doesn't matter to me at all," were his first words. He turned his face and body to Elisabeth and looked her in the eye. "I honestly wouldn't give a damn if we had polkadot children, I would love them just the same," he smiled, clearly having given the matter deep thought on the drive back to London.

How weak you are Mark, Elisabeth thought.

To him she said: "Have you even wondered if that old witch was telling the truth about me? Having seen my reputation ruined in front of the most important people in our future, wouldn't you even be interested in finding out what lies behind her lie?"

Her words were strong and she didn't care. She sighed and more tears came.

"Oh Elisabeth, don't take it like that. I know Mama would be furious, but she can't continue trying to live my life. I just don't care and I mean it." Mark was serious.

Elisabeth signed again. 'Thanks Mark. I know you mean it in the best way." She opened the car door and started getting out.

"Whatever that woman said, I'm determined to get to the bottom of it. I'm going to do some research, because I may need to take legal action against her, and maybe even your mother too." Mark sat upright. "Don't worry Mark. It's not time for that yet. It's time I spent some time with my family. They'll be glad to see me."

"You want me to drive you there tomorrow?" Mark was eager to please.

"No," Elisabeth was sure. "I'll take the train and have Johnson meet me at the station."

"How long will you be gone for?"

"Who knows?" was all Elisabeth could answer.

Before her eyes floated a fresh memory of the walls and walls of oil paintings in the formal rooms of her own family's stately home, portrait-filled scenes of three hundred years of proud family history frozen in time on huge canvases by illustrious and renowned artists, hung high on the walls of many vaulted rooms in the mansion. The paintings had been ignored in her childhood and then accepted as she grew into adulthood and understood them as relics of a past that explained, or at least justified, the expensive residence and unlimited wealth of her family.

The artistic history was well recorded in volumes of books and ancient documents that she had never read, stored in the estate library with its wall-to-ceiling collection of important literature, and the live-in historian Everald Howe who had made the library his special spot to add to the History degree he had received from Oxford, before being recruited by Elisabeth's family to establish and operate a school for the village children.

"Yes," Elisabeth smiled, re-energized as she dragged her suitcase upstairs to her flat, ready to re-fill it with a new set of clothes. "I will go home."

CHAPTER SIXTEEN

MARIE

KINGSTON, JAMAICA – 1972

Was that an ant biting? Marie pushed down the foot of socks below her ankle and found the small black spot crawling further down, grabbed it with two fingers, crushing it at the same time and flung it away from her. She adjusted her skirt and smoothed it under her, then shifted further down into the comfortable crook of the tree in whose lower branches she sat.

She looked down at the small Timex watch on her left wrist. Quarter to five... this is longer than usual. She could hear sounds coming from the back of the big old house in the big yard with its many shady trees, sounds of happy male laughter, sometimes the sound of a guitar or two, and men's voices singing.

"I bet he's smoking ganja too," Marie thought. Her brother Marshall who was supposed to accompany her home from her day's classes and who stopped at this big old house every afternoon, could only be stopping there to do what all the men in the yard were doing – smoking ganja. She knew they did it, because they didn't hide their long, white ganja cigars from her sight when they passed her walking in, out or around the yard. They would acknowledge the girl waiting with her school bag under the tree, with a slight bow and a tip of a forefinger to the forehead, usually with the hand holding the cigar.

Marie knew the manners her mother had taught her, and nodded her head. Marie was 18, just finished high school with good passes in English, Maths, General Knowledge and Domestic Science. Her mother, Altherine Grant, was proud enough to move her from her grandmother's humble St. Elizabeth board house, to live with her in the maid's room at the back of the house in the uptown part of Kingston where she worked as a live-in domestic maid.

The maids room was big enough for another small bed for Marie, and the money Altherine used to send to help Gran feed Marie and send her to school, she now invested in sending her to university so she could eventually get 'a proper job'.

But she wanted to make sure her daughter was safe alone on Kingston's streets at rush hour, so Marie waited for her brother with obedience, but annoyance.

Marie's gratitude at her mother's sacrifice ensured she was diligent in her studies. She loved being in Kingston, so modern with proper streets not just dirt roads like St. Elizabeth. There were cars on the roads, shops you could buy things in and buses so you didn't have to walk home, so she was a little annoyed this afternoon at being kept waiting yet again by her brother. What could it be that so attracted him to these men and this place? She wondered.

Marie opened her bag and took out the 'newspaper' that had been pushed into her hands at the Students Union. Six pages printed on a stencil machine containing articles, poems, quotes and comments about the world Black Power movement.

She liked these publications with news about people she could hardly believe existed, a breed of Black people who were fighting a new kind of war with words and books to change the minds of Black people to realize the truth of their African history. And a war against those who have caused the history of black people to be so full of pain, sorrow and death ... the people of Europe.

It was good to have such literary company as she waited. Was there really a Black revolution coming where people were going to 'fight for their rights'? How did you fight like that? Did she understand the cause properly?

"Ready?" It was Marshall, dragging on a cap and his book bag.

"Long time." She paused and looked at him. "What is it really, that makes you have to stop here every day, Marshall?"

"The MUSIC, Marie, the MUSIC!" he smiled as they walked home. "One day you will understand."

*   *   *   *

Another day. Marie sighed again, as she stepped out the door and turned the key in the lock. She took a deep, fresh breath of the outside yard before walking along the tree-covered pathway from her mother's maid's room behind the three-bedroom family home that occupied the spacious, flower-filled yard in front. It was not a short walk to the campus, but it was her daily exercise and she walked briskly with her head held high and shoulders braced back by the bookbag.

She walked along the neat pavement that ringed the neighbourhood, then cut through a dirt pathway edged by knee-high grasses that wound under the shade of several guango trees until it finally met up with the campus Ring Road. Marie thought about her life and what she could do to end the total boredom she felt about everything in her existence.

First, there were her university studies for her B.A. in English with a minor in Communications. Marie felt she knew so much more than the other students in her class; they were slow to understand the lessons, hated to have to learn the superiority of English literature and language over their lazy perfection of the Jamaican patois, until they had realized they were unemployable without it.

Marie was glad she studied speaking English, like her mother told her she had to speak in her job in the big house in Kingston. She liked listening to the speech patterns of radio announcers and especially the newsreaders. Every school day was an exercise in frustration and practice in keeping her temper, not screaming and tearing her hair out as she listened to the Professor vainly trying to drag the majority through the courses in the allocated time.

Marie knew she would pass her final English exams and receive her degree. It bored her to have to continue going to classes every day. She had had enough of 'school' and education. After passing seven CXCs at High School, she had wanted to spend at least a year working and earning money for university. But her mother had insisted she go straight to university and get her degree, so Marie's excellent grades and her mother's extreme poverty had qualified her for a student loan that helped pay for her tuition.

Marie's mother was a problem in her life. Not that Maria did not love her mother. Maria loved her mother Altherine Grant more than anything in her life. Maria had never known a father and her mother had never had any more children after her second 'mistake', raising Maria and Marshall herself on the smalls she could earn selling the produce from the garden behind the wattle-and-daub house they lived in on land that had been in the Grant family for two generations.

Marie was born in 1952 in a small seaside home near Little Bay. She attended St. Elizabeth Secondary School, graduated in 1970 and was in her first year of University. When Marie was a little girl, she had once asked her mother why they had to live in such a broken-down, old-fashioned house. That was the first time Altherine had told her that they were fortunate to have land they could prove belonged to their family and a house that she did not have to pay rent or mortgage for. It was the first of many times she would tell Marie the history of the Grant family.

She would tell her about her Great-Great Grandmother, born 1819 on the Worthy Park Plantation, who died in 1834 when the Sam Sharpe Rebellion spread across the island from St. James to St. Catherine, accused of being one of the plotters and hanged afterwards as one of more than 200 slaves who were punished, when all she was doing was just going to the Baptist church to hear Sam Sharpe preach.

She told her the stories her mother and her grandmother had told her about her family, how her great grandmother Elly escaped with her grandmother Nicey to Sligoville, to hide from the soldiers and Maroons that were searching to capture and deliver them to the hangman's nooses at Montego Bay and St. Jago de la Vega.

She told Marie how they hid in the hills with the other runaways for four years, living like the Maroons among those Maroons who refused to be conscripted into the militia, until the news of Emancipation spread across the island and those in hiding could come down from the hills and live like their fellow freedmen.

She told her how Elly an Nicey got work as cane cutters and weeders on the Worthy Park sugar estate which earned them the right to mark out a plot of land on the hillsides, along with other sugar workers, land that became a 'free village' for the slaves freed by Emancipation.

Altherine made Marie proud of the little house set on a corner of the family land, surrounded by its vegetable garden, sticks of yam, lines of okras, beds of lettuce and plump tomatoes. She knew her mother had been sad to leave the land that fed them, to go to Kingston and take work as a helper so she could earn to buy Marie and her brother school uniforms, shoes and books every year until they finally passed their high school exams. She knew her mother was glad Marie was now in Kingston living with her. But living with her mother was not what Marie wanted in life.

Marie sighed as she pulled her book bag up off her back and slung its weight over her left arm, it's flaps and zips making a 'face' of its oval canvas shape that seemed to stare accusingly as her for her lateness on its designated journey to the University campus.

But Marie knew that simply having a university degree was not enough to ensure a job in the notoriously exclusive Kingston job market, where one's home address and social upbringing meant more than the high pass marks of a rural high school graduate. Yet, without a job it would be impossible for Marie and her mother to live on their own in Kingston. With the student loan coming to an end, some other means would have to be found to support Marie in Kingston.

These were just two of the problems that caused Marie to be bored and frustrated with her life. It wasn't fair. She stamped the dust off her shoes as she stepped onto the asphalted university road and crossed to the outdoor food court where she bought her daily box of orange juice. She sat down on an empty bench, and zipped open her book bag to extract her notebook. Pen poised over a clean page, she waited for the inspiration that guided her daily comments to herself. One day, she smiled, these notes will become my autobiography.

"Hi Marie!" It was Joseph, the campus nerd who always found a reason to chat with her.

"What's up, Joseph?"

Marie pressed the button on her ballpoint, giving Joseph her smile. At least Joseph was a diversion from her unruly thoughts.

"There was someone asking for you earlier," Joseph informed. "A girl, saying she wanted to know if she could do some research in the Library on the Grant family."

Marie was surprised and interested. "Why is she searching for information about Grants?"

"Don't know," replied Joseph. "I told her to ask Mrs. Pierce, the librarian, to help her and she went over there."

Marie picked up her book bag and returned her notebook and pen to its dark interior. "Let me go find her. Maybe I can help. What's she wearing, so I can identify her."

"Oh no problem identifying her," Joseph laughed. "She will be the only blonde, white woman talking with Mrs. Pierce."

Then, as Marie started immediately towards the Library, he shouted after her "She looks rich. You owe me a lunch!"

Marie paused as she entered the Library. Looking around the vast rows of books and desks with students' heads bent over books, Marie saw the girl immediately. But instead of going over to Mrs. Pierce's desk, she walked away until a shelf of books hid her, from behind which she peeped out.

The girl was about Marie's age, white with blonde hair that was casually clasped into a pony tail by an elastic band. She wore leather hiking sandals and khaki trousers with a short-sleeved white shirt. The only indication of wealth was a leather handbag slung over her shoulder that bore the unmistakable double-C signature of Channel couture.

Hmmm, thought Marie. Wonder what this is about!

Time to find out.

She walked over to Mrs. Pierce's desk as if she had just gotten up from a study table, book bag in hand.

"Morning Mrs. Pierce. Did you get the Roger Mais novel *'Brother Man'* back yet? I just need to check something." She smiled at Mrs. Pierce.

"Hi Marie. No, I haven't got back any of my copies yet. Seems all you English undergrads want to check something in that book before exams. You'll have to check me back later," Mrs. Pierce explained.

"But," Mrs. Pierce continued, "I'm glad to see you right now. This young lady is researching the Grant family and since you're a Grant, maybe you can help her." Turning to the girl standing at her desk, she said: "Marie, this is Elizabeth Grant, from England. Elizabeth, this is Marie Grant."

Marie stretched out her hand and it was clasped as firmly as she held the slim white hand in hers. Two blue eyes looked into her dark brown eyes with a gentle smile and a very English voice said "From a Grant to a Grant, I'm really glad to meet a Grant at last. Can we go somewhere and talk, please."

They sat on a bench under the spreading guango tree facing the Library, with the beautiful Blue Mountains framing the flowering lawns of the University. Marie didn't want to stare, but it was hard not to keep looking at the very pink skin and very blonde hair and very blue eyes of the girl who sat beside her, saying she was a Grant.

"Yes, I am a Grant and I hope we are related," Elizabeth smiled and took one of Marie's hands in her own. Marie pulled it away as if she had been stuck with a pin.

"I don't see HOW you and I could be related!" Marie was shocked.

"Why? Because I have pink skin with yellow hair and you have brown skin and wooly black hair?" Elizabeth smiled. "Why not?"

"Why not? I would describe it as the very remote possibility of a child of the slave- master and a child of a slave being related," said Marie after thinking for a moment. "I mean, you and I could have the same last name because the slave masters used to give his slaves his last name, to show he owned them. I know that's how my family is named Grant, for my great, great, great grandmother was named Grant when she ran away from Busha Grant's Frome estate to Sligoville in the 1834 Revolution."

"Sounds like you really know some history. You're going to be a great help," Elizabeth smiled.

Marie was still not happy. "So you mean you are looking for your slave-master ancestors – the ones that used to own my ancestors? Find their graves and lay some flowers and such? Did they have some brown-skin, pretty hair bastard children they left to grow up in Jamaica? Is that why are you looking for the Jamaican Grants? You have something for them?"

"You mean, like money?" Elizabeth's smile grew wider. "No, I am not looking for them to give them any money. In fact, maybe they have something to give me."

Marie was surprised. "What could that be?"

"I'm looking for the history of the Grant family. I knew I would find an intelligent person if I started at the university. Will you help me?"

"The Grant family history? You want me to help you find it? Depends on what we have to look for, where we have to look, how long it will take us to find it, all of that. You will have to have some money. I am not taking the bus. And I eat proper food, three meals a day." Marie crossed her arms on her chest.

Elizabeth smiled. "I drive. I have rented a car. I have enough money to feed us and pay for hotel rooms if we have to sleep while we are on the road. I want a chief researcher. I can even pay you a small fee." She smiled again.

Marie looked at her smiling face and thought. How long could it take to track down some Grant family history to satisfy this tourist girl, Marie asked herself. A weekend, a few days maybe, some long driving, road food and maybe even a North Coast hotel to experience for the first time. And get paid too!!

She would tell her mother she got a drive down to see Grandma in Sligoville, and her mother would be glad to give her some soap and matches and tinned things to carry for Grandma.

"Ready?" Elizabeth took out some keys from her purse. "Come. I am parked over here."

'You mean, start right NOW?" Marie was astonished.

"Why not, your exams are not till next week. Let's go get your bag and tell your family. I don't have much time in Jamaica." The girl was serious.

Marie looked at her Elisabeth seriously. She looked back into Maria's eyes with a purity of intent and clean spirit, that Marie realized she could be trusted. She suddenly felt like a caretaker for this trusting white girl, whom she knew she had to protect while she searched for what she wanted and needed to find.

"Ok, I'll come with you. Let's go. I have to tell my mother. She will tell me I have to bring my brother with us. She won't let me go alone."

"That's OK. It would be good protection for us to have a man with us." Elisabeth smiled and nodded.

Marie smiled ruefuly. "You don't know my brother!"

As they walked across the parking lot, Marie gave her a last chance to say this was all a joke. "So why are we *really* looking for the Grants, Elisabeth?" she asked.

For the first moment since their meeting each other, the smile left Elisabeth's face and it became serious. She stopped and looked Marie straight in the eyes.

"I want to find my slave ancestors," she answered.

CHAPTER EIGHTEEN

LOOKING FOR MERCY

"All I have is this photo of the first painting in our family gallery." Elisabeth   opened a notebook and took out a colour photograph of a painting. "This is my great, great, I don't know how many 'greats', grandfather Captain James Grant. He was a merchant sailor, a captain. It could have been a slave ship, and I'm sure he made one or two trips to Africa. But I'm sure he wasn't a slaver, I know he made his money on bringing goods to the island, like food, salted meat, cloth, nails, shoes, lanterns, ..."

"And slave chains and a gibbet or two, I'm also sure." Marie's voice was dry, lips pursed.

The two girls were sitting on the balcony of a modest guest house in Uptown Kingston, where Elisabeth was staying. It was midday and the remains of a traditional Jamaican lunch lay resting on the table between them.

"Ok, you're probably right." Elisabeth held hands up in surrender pose. "But look ... let's not argue about the history of black and white yet. Let's just trace the story. I mean, if he was an evil slave captain, who was this wife of his who is supposed to be my Black ancestor? This is the portrait commemorating his receiving the earldom 1776 as Viscount Falmouth. His Viscountess was supposed to be a Black slave, or that's what I was told."

She placed the photo before Marie. The painting was of an aristocratic English couple standing before a column of marble draped with a royal blue cloth. In the background was a scene of English countryside, fields and meadows, a large tree under which two sleek dogs rested. A tall white man wearing a wig of curled gray hair that fell onto his shoulders stood in the center. He wore a long back coat that reached to his knees, with a pale blue waistcoat that covered a white shirt with frilled sleeves and a white cravat peeking out from under. His trousers were knee britches worn over blue stockings, with shoes with pointy toes and a silver buckle.

Beside him stood a white woman, wearing a wide hoop-skirted gown of pink and red brocade. A deep plunging neckline was tied with red lace and around her neck was a choker of jewels. Her skin was pale, slightly paler even than her husband's. But it was her hair that commanded attention. A pile of honey-coloured curls tumbled from her head to her shoulders, falling gently over one bosom.

"What a beautiful woman. Who was she?" Maria asked.

"According to the records, she is the first Viscountess." Elisabeth explained. "Her name was Mercy, and she came from Jamaica."

"That's who you here to look for?" Marie considered this fact for a moment. How do you know she was Black? A lot of white women were born in Jamaica, children of slavemasters. She must be one of them."

Marie thought some more. "Maybe the rumour she was Black could have come if she had brought a slave with her from Jamaica and ..."

"That's one thing I thought," Elisabeth interrupted. "Maybe the lord of the manor felt it his right to impregnate the slave, even though he had a wife at home, and that's how the rumour started. But there is no record of any Black slave living on our estate from then or since." Elisabeth nodded. "And she had 5 children with him, all of whom seem to have been White. So it was clearly a long-term relationship."

"So you are sure this is her, a Jamaican slave? And you want to find her."

"Yes." Elisabeth's tone was strong. "I never really thought about my 'ancestors' before this. They were just some long gone folks with records that you can trace for many generations, who gave birth to the people who gave birth to me. Bit of a handicap, to be true, in this day and age, this so-called 'privilege'. Being an aristocrat is not all it's made out to be. Very restricting, and sometimes even dangerous." She smiled.

"But I found something very interesting when I was trying to find out more about my family." Out of her bag she pulled a small book.

"It's a book about Black Europeans, men and women. Not just African slaves, but people who lived in Europe as free Europeans. I found there were quite a few women. There was Queen Charlotte of England, the wife of George III, who many say definitely has African features. Queen Charlotte's race has long been a matter of controversy because if so, then the Royal Family has some Black blood too."

Marie smiled at the thought.

"There was Queen Charlotte of Mecklenburg-Stelitz," Elisabeth continued, "who is of partial German descent. She is also said to descend from a African branch of the Portuguese royal family by way of Magarita de Castro e Souza, a 15th-century Portuguese noblewoman, who are said to be Moors and therefore of African descent."

"The most famous story of all is about Dido Belle," Elisabeth leaned forward to explain. "She was the brown-skinned daughter of a Scottish naval commander and his slave mistress and she lived in London in the late 1790s.

"She wasn't a slave, she was free. What is most interesting about her is that she was brought up in the family of her uncle, the first Earl of Mansfield who was also the Chief Justice of England. There's a famous painting of her and another of his nieces, the very white Lady Elizabeth Murray with both of them dressed in nice clothes and clearly living happily together as equals.

"What caused Dido Belle's story to become famous, is that Lord Mansfield presided over two landmark cases to do with slavery and his judgment in both of them did a lot to bring about the abolition of slavery." She smiled at Marie's surprised expression.

"Yes, people said that Dido Belle's presence in Lord Mansfield's home was the chief influence in his judgments," she added with another smile. "Can you imagine a Black woman with so much power or influence in those times!"

"Hmmm." Marie was intrigued. "How did she come to be living in his house?"

"She had her own money." Elisabeth explained. "She was grand-niece of a politically connected aristocrat who left her his fortune, and even Lord Mansfield left her money in his will. So you see, there were quite a few women of colour in Britain in those days."

"So there were others." Marie shook her head. "Black and White certainly mixed it up, didn't they, from long ago! Still doing it too!" She smiled. "I didn't realize that."

Marie rubbed her chin and looked at the picture again. "But this woman definitely does not look Black! Look at her hair! I just can't believe that someone with blonde hair could be Black."

"Blonde hair has always been a feature of the women of my family." Elizabeth pulled on her golden yellow ponytail. "Other blondes go brown as they get older, but in our family we stay blonde till we get gray! Mother used to say that to me sometimes, when she brushed my hair."

"So that's going to make it even harder, looking for a white Black woman who lived 200 years ago somewhere in Jamaica! Not going to be easy." Marie shook her head. "There were not many, that's the best part, but finding them will be like looking for a needle in a haystack!"

Marie folded her arms on her chest and took a deep breath.

She thought about it for a while, then said: "Le's go for a drive and look for my grandmother. She is the closest person I know to slavery. She was a young girl when it ended and her mother helped set up the first village for free Africans after Abolition, up at a place called Sligoville. She might have some stories and advice."

"Where will we find her? I'm ready." Elisabeth picked up her purse and got up from the table.

"The village where she lives is up in the hills above Kingston. Let's put some gas in your car, then stop by my brother to work out our travel plans for tomorrow."

*   *   *   *

Elisabeth and Marie were silent as the car drove through the Kingston after-work traffic up the twists and turns of the Red Hills road up into the St.

Andrew hills. The light of the reddening sunset
turned the sky gold, then dark blue as night began its
embrace. Soon Elisabeth turned on the car's
headlight and drove more slowly and carefully. Then
Elisabeth finally spoke.

"They certainly hate me. All white people."
Elisabeth finally spoke, gripping the steering wheel as
hard as she gritted her teeth.

"No, they don't hate you. Just your English
history. Seems like you don't know much about it!"

Marie knew she would have to deal with
Elisabeth's emotions following the meeting they had
just had with her brother and the other members of
the band who they would be traveling with. No one
was pleased to learn that they had to take two girls
with them on their first serious job as a band,
following a politician across the island and playing
music at public meetings to drum up support for an
upcoming election.

Worse, that one of them was White. The
Whirlwind Band prided itself on being the militant
musical voice of those Jamaicans just beginning to
learn about the history of English slavery in Jamaica,

and to express their anger at all that reminded them of that past. To have to be close to someone who represented all they were opposed to and expressed in song and lifestyle, had caused the meeting to be an explosion of angry comments.

"They don't know my history, dammit!." Elisabeth slapped the steering wheel and the car swerved for a moment into the bushes at the roadside.

"Carefull! " Marie shouted. "Now you see why it's best we travel with them in their bus. You can't drive these roads."

"I am a perfectly good driver and I was perfectly happy to drive my rental," Elisabeth was angry, "I don't want to drive with them if they don't want me anywhere near them, because of the colour of my skin!"

"Stop being so emotional" Marie smiled. "Now you know what it's like for Black people sometimes, eh? You got a taste of the racism we have to put up with in your White country! We hear all about it from our relatives who live in England. Racism is the worst thing, they say, worse than winter. You are going to find a lot of reactions like that in Jamaica, so get used to it and learn to ignore it, like we Black people have to ignore it when it happens to us!"

"You mean everyone in Jamaica hates white people! If I had known, I wouldn't have bothered to come all this way!" Elisabeth was angry.

"Never mind." Marie tried to soothe Elisabeth's anger. "Not everyone is like my brother and his friends. And they don't hate you. They're just angry at having to take women along with them. Tomorrow we will give back this car and travel with them in their bus. The money you save on the car we will use to pay for gas and food on the road, and you will still save money."

"What was his name, the one that asked if I was 'Queen *Eliza-bitch*'?" Elisabeth's lips were set tight.

Marie laughed. "That was Tony, he's the lead singer. Don't mind him. He's always angry. That's what his songs are about ... anger at Babylon, as they call the world, the System. I had to smile when he said that. Look, I will lend you one of the student newspapers they distribute on campus when we get back to the city. It can explain some of what they think better than I can."

"Why do their wear their hair like that? Uncombed. Is that because they can't afford combs, or just to scare white people? Because it certainly scares me!" Elisabeth continued driving.

"They call that hair dreadlocks ... they say the Mau Mau warriors in Kenya used to wear their hair like that. They call themselves 'Rasta' and they say that the Emperor of Ethiopia is God!" Marie answered. "That's all I really know about it."

"So these are the madmen you want me to spend a week with in the middle of the Jamaican jungle! People who don't believe in God!!! I must be crazy to agree to this!" Elisabeth looked ahead at the road.

Marie still smiled. "They aren't mad. They are an expression of Black identity that has been happening more and more in Jamaica since we started hearing about Black Power, and 'Black is Beautiful', and Angela Davis, and Malcolm X and all that stuff happening in America. We have also been learning about the teachings of our first National Hero – a man named Marcus Garvey, who preached race pride and said that we Black people should stop trying to be like our European former slavemasters and identify ourselves and culture with Africa. Some people say this is a racist philosophy of people who want to start a revolution, so it's not exactly popular with the Uptown people. But the people who think like that make good music that people like to listen to and dance to, so that kind of music is becoming very popular."

"I was hearing about 'Black is Beautiful' in England." Elisabeth relaxed a little . "I went to the Supremes concert at the Albert Hall. They were good. So these guys sing their revolution? Like Bob Dylan?" Elisabeth could think of no other comparison.

"Who is Bob Dylan?" Marie was puzzled. "These guys are more like singing Black Panthers, if you know who they are."

"And what was that about we girls have to be wearing skirts and covering our heads to travel with them? What was that about?" Elisabeth was still angry.

"Yes, we have to accept their rules of how women around them should dress. They say pants are men's clothing, and that good women cover their heads in public."

"Why? Is this the Middle East?"

"Jamaican country women mostly wear skirts and dresses too, scarves and hats to cover their heads when they are on the road. You know, church clothes. They go to church a lot." Marie was apprehensive. "Didn't you bring any skirts with you?"

Elisabeth sighed. "I have a khaki skirt, but the rest are just evening clothes I wouldn't wear on the road."

"Well good thing it's khaki, because you will be wearing it for a week. You have a scarf to tie your head?"

"The skirt has a matching sunhat. I brought them to wear in the jungle."

Marie laughed. "You won't find much jungle in Jamaica, so wear it on the road to cover your head. They can't complain."

"I'm not looking forward to this at all." Elisabeth was resigned. "How much further to your Grandma's house?"

"We're nearly there. Take the next road on the left and it's just another minute."

The narrow road was more stones than asphalt. The lights of the car showed a few small houses set far apart, small old buildings set on blocks elevating them from the ground, with steps upwards to small verandahs edged in lattice work. Dogs lay on front steps, chickens scratched in yards, mango and orange trees gave shade.

"This one up there on the right. Slow down here." Marie pointed and Elisabeth slowed down and stopped in front of a house set behind a hedge of red hibiscus.

"Follow me. Let me do most of the talking." They got out of the car and Marie led Elisabeth down the path, but instead of walking up onto the verandah, turned right and walked around to the back of the house calling out:

.   "Gran! Gran! Grandma! It's me!!!"

The dogs started barking, running up to her, scaring Elisabeth who grabbed Marie's arm, then realized from her wide smile that all was safe and, holding on, follower her.

"Gran! I come to visit you!"

A young girl came out from the back of the house. She wore an apron and had a big spoon in her hand.

"Oh, is you, Miss Marie!" She waved at Marie, then turned back into the house shouting "Miss Nicey! Miss Marie come visit you! Miss Nicey!!"

Marie led Elisabeth into the small house, walking through the cluttered kitchen where plantains were frying a small coal stove, into the main room of the house divided by furniture into a dining room with table and chairs, then a living room with sofa, armchairs and side-tables. Here, by the light of a kerosene Home Sweet Home lamp, sat Marie's grandmother, Miss Nicey Grant.

Miss Nicey was dark brown like coffee. Her head was wrapped in a cotton scarf and she wore a loose house-dress, white socks and slippers. Her smile showed she was missing her upper front teeth and a stick rested beside her in the armchair.

The old lady raised herself up halfway out of an armchair and embraced Marie with a big smile.

"You come look fi you Granny! Mi blessed gran'dawta! Give me a kiss!!"

The two embraced. "How you Modda?"

"She alright, Gran, she sen' something for you." She reached into the bag she was carrying and brought out a paper bag.

"See some Liptons Tea, some crackers and 2 big tins of bully beef." The love between the two shone on their faces.

"Come, sit down. Long time me no see you!" She patted the sofa beside her.

"I bring a frien' to meet you, Gran" Marie turned to introduce Elisabeth and her grandmother's face lit up even more brightly.

"You bring this pretty little white girl come visit me! Is who she? Come, hug me up!" She stretched out her arms and, Elisabeth – smiling at the warmth of the welcome – bent over and hugged the old lady.

"This is my friend Elisabeth, Gran. She is at university with me."

"Nice to meet you pretty girl. You welcome, welcome. Come here!" Miss Nicey reached out to touch Elisabeth's hair. "Look at her hair! Just like a dolly!"

Elisabeth smiled.

"Gran, we come to talk to you." Marie sat down and signaled Elisabeth to sit beside her. "We need your help with some work we are doing at the University. We're trying to find out some more about slavery, and you are the only person I know who knows about slavery, so we come to ask you about it."

"Slavery? Me no like talk 'bout slavery days." Miss Nicey's face soured. "Too much bad things go on in slavery."

"Yes, but sometimes you have to remember the bad things to make good things happen. You and your mother did something good. You were some of the people who set up this village as a place for free slaves to make a home after Emancipation. That was a very good thing that came out of slavery, because the village is still here. And so are you."

"I agree with you, that was good." Miss Nicey nodded. "But not much else was good. We didn't get no money for it. Still don't have no money. Poor same way. Look at this bruk-down place we live. You show me something good!"

Marie leaned over to her Gran.

"Suppose I was to tell you that Elisabeth and I are related!"

Miss Nicey was shocked.

"WHAT!!! You joking, girl! That is not possible! Stop tell me lie! You not too big for me to beat you."

Marie laughed. "Maybe related to you too!"

Miss Nicey put a hand on the stick resting beside her, then decided not to pick it up.

"How?" Miss Nicey looked from Elisabeth's white face to her grand-daughter's brown face.

"That is what we want to find out. She is a Grant from England, says we could be the same family, coming from slavery times. We want to track down the links and see if it's true." Marie replied.

"I remember you used to tell me that your mother said her mother Amina had a sister who had a daughter with yellow hair, that was taken away and she never saw her again. I remember one night you told me a story of the girl with yellow hair."

Miss Nicey sat back and remembered. "Lawd yes, I remember mi Mother used to tell me story about a girl with yellow hair.... not the only one ... said it used to happen all the time ... the Massa would take a slave and the baby girl would come out pretty ... couldn't make her work in the field ... couldn't bring her into the Great House ... so she would get sold quick, quick."

"So, how can I find out if that woman you remember was one of my ancestors?" Elisabeth spoke anxiously.

"Well, I don't know how." Miss Nicey thought. "That plantation that my grandmother slave on not there any more. Turn into a banana farm now."

"Where was it?"

"Near Falmouth. They used to grow sugar cane, but after Emancipation they sold it, and then someone else buy it and sell parts of it, and the new owner in the banana business now."

"I know they used to keep records of slave sales on every plantation. Where would I find the records for that plantation? We have to find them" Elisabeth was eager to know.

"If it was in Falmouth, we have to check the records at the Trelawny Parish Council," Marie explained. "We can do that when we drive through Falmouth with the band; we can go and check the office there."

Miss Nicey was curious. "Why you want to find out if you and me is relative? You love black people?"

Elisabeth laughed. "Yes, I do, Miss Nicey. But it's more than that. I want to find out about myself."

"Well I hope you don't find out that you Black. That not good at all. Stay white." Miss Nicey pursed her lips.

"Gran! How can you say that?" Marie was not ready to accept that.

"Nothing good ever happen to Black people yet." She turned her head away.   "All that happen to Black people is suffering and poverty and hatred. Nobody want to be Black. Don't bother fill up this nice lady head with any Black nonsense like I hear them a-talk 'bout on the radio. Just make her stay white an' pretty!"

Elisabeth covered her smile with her hand, then looked at Marie and giggled. Marie, who was both shocked and embarrassed, started to make an answer for her grandmother's comments, then thought better of the argument that would follow and sat back in the sofa with a resigned sigh.

"There was a man here once, not long ago," Miss Nicey continued. "He tried to do something for Black people ... make a new village and run it like in Africa ... Black people living happy together ... helping each other ... not far from here ... just up that hill ... him call the place Pinnacle. They fight him hard ... mash up the people houses, burn down their crops, run him off of him land ...nearly kill him."

Miss Nicey's voice was strong. "Mr. Howell him did name.... I remember him good-good. That was the

last man tried to do something good for Black people.
Where is he now? Madhouse, I hear. Don't want to
hear nothing about slavery times. Bad, bad."

She picked up her stick and stood up on shaky
legs and shouted. "Beryl!"

The girl cooking in the kitchen came in and
Miss Nicey gave her the bag Marie had brought with
her. Then she insisted that the girls stay and eat some
bully beef and crackers with her and drink some tea,
even though Marie protested that she had brought the
food for Miss Nicey, not for them to eat it all up!

"Please give her this money when we're
leaving?" Elisabeth whispered in Marie's ear, pressing
some paper notes in her hand. Marie was glad to add
the English Pounds to the Ten Jamaican Dollars her
mother had given her for Miss Nicey.

It was not until later, as Elisabeth steered the
car carefully back down the hill, that she spoke about
Miss Nicey's view on race.

"She has lived in slavery, but she thinks White
people are better. But your brother's friends have
been born free-- the bass guitarist Rupert even looks

mixed with White blood – yet they hate White people! How come opinions are so different?"

"That's a hard one to understand, for me too." Marie gave the matter some thought. "If you think about it, the way the country got sorted out after slavery, Whites still control, give out the jobs, own the big houses, run the country. I can understand how someone who has lived all their life under that system just accepts it, can't think it can ever change. That's what I think makes my grandmother think like she does."

"But I only see Black people around me in Jamaica, hardly any Whites! Black people seem to be in control."

"Yes, but look at the people in the newspaper ads, look at the people in the TV shows and the commercials, look at the people in the movies ... everything is White or near White. Even the Miss Jamaica beauty queens have to be either White or nearly White. So the older generation has grown up in that way of thinking and they are the majority viewpoint. You see what I mean?"

"Yes I see what you mean." Elisabeth nodded.

Marie continued. "But on the other hand, the young generation is fighting against that because they are learning more about our history, about Africa and about Black people and about slavery, about the terrible things White people did to Black people in slavery. So instead of loving White like your Gran, they hate everything about White. You see?"

"Yes. In a nutshell."

The two drove in silence for a long while, before Elisabeth spoke again.

"Well I see it's going to be a very interesting journey."

CHAPTER NINETEEN

ON THE ROAD

The bus was a middle-aged Volkswagen painted blue – clearly a home job, as the brush marks were evident. The rear back fender was scraped down to the rusty metal in a first attempt to repair the effects of a collision. Same for the front left side which also had a dented fender to confirm a previous connection with a hard object. The bus pulled up in front of the guest house where Marie and Elizabeth waited, the horn blowing loudly.

Marie sighed, then strengthened her shoulders, picked up her two bags and turned to Elisabeth. "Let's go."

Elisabeth followed her to the bus with her bags and a look of apprehension. A panel door slid sideways, exposing the interior of the bus containing four dread-locksed young men.

In the drivers front seat sat Jacob, the band's drummer, his big body squeezed behind the steering wheel. He turned and nodded to Marie. Beside him sat Tony, the lead singer, tall and skinny with his short locks squashed underneath a black tam, looking steadfastly out the windscreen and not acknowledging the girls.

There were two bench seats in the body of the bus. Marshall, Marie's brother sat on the first bench seat with Rupert, the bass player who sat by the window examining the street as if there was something interesting outside. The second bench was empty.

Marshall jumped off and helped the girls lift their bags into the bus, pushing them onto and under the second seat and helping the girls get in. The back space of the bus was filled with instruments – a drum set, two guitar bags, and an assortment of suitcases and bags, a bunch of coconuts, worn shoes and a football.

"Ok. Ready for the road!" Marshall gave a smile, which Elisabeth gratefully returned. Marie was serious-faced.

"Yes, let's go."

"First, we gotta get some gas, then some breakfast." Marshall had clearly taken charge, as the others continued to show their displeasure at having the girls travel with them.

Jacob drove the bus into a gas station and Elisabeth pulled out her credit card. "Fill it up."

Jacob turned to look at her, all of them watching the transaction with eyes wide open, clearly not accustomed to such generosity and evidence of wealth. Paying the bill with Elisabeth's card took some of the edge off the girls' presence, but not much.

And not for long.

"Where can we get breakfast?" Elisabeth asked, proud that the display of her wealth seemed to break the icy silence in the bus. "Is there somewhere we can get some bacon and eggs?"

The bus screeched to a halt and four angry black faces turned the full volume of hatred to Elisabeth.

"Bacon!"

"Pig!"

"Swine food!!!"

"Yu mus' be crazy!" Four voices shouted all at once.

"What did I do wrong?" Elisabeth recoiled from their angry shouts.

"Eating pig is the worst thing you could have suggested." Marie tried to explain. "Rasta say pigs are unclean."

"Is not Rasta say that. The Bible say that swine is unclean, we must not eat it." Marshall explained. "That's a BIG insult for you to invite Rasta to eat pig. We not traveling with you if you going to eat pig!!!"

"I'm so sorry!" Elisabeth blushed with embarrassment. "I didn't know! I'm so sorry!!"

Marie jumped to her rescue. "Don't be so hard on her. She didn't know!"

From the front seat, Tony spoke without turning his head.

"I knew we shouldn't agree to drive with this slave-master daughter. She goin' jinx this trip, I tell you that!" He slapped the dashboard with a stick he carried that was painted red, yellow and green. "Slave and slave-master children don't mix!"

"Look, I am not a slave master." Elisabeth was no longer apologetic, but angry. "Neither are you a slave. It's not going to be a good trip if that's how you are going to see me."

Tony turned and fixed his eyes directly into Elisabeth's. They were red as if they were on fire. "You don't know your history! You don't even read Bible! You don't know that your ancestors enslaved my ancestors?"

"Yes, I know something about slavery," Elisabeth was prepared to meet the challenge head on. "But not every White person you meet today was a slave-master's child. You can't dismiss every White person by saying they are slave-masters. That was 300 years ago and slavery ended more than 100 years ago. Maybe it's YOU who don't know your history."

"I don't know history! You rude!!" Tony was irate. "Look around you and see how poor Jamaica is, compared with your rich and lovely Great Britain. See if you don't see the difference! You White people got rich by enslaving us Black people. You built up your country on the blood, sweat and tears of my people for three hundred years. Your cities like Liverpool and Bristol and Manchester got rich from my people's suffering. See if you see any Black people rich like you in England. How many Jamaicans you think can buy gas with a piece of plastic?"

"Not many can, and not many in England can either," Elisabeth replied defiantly. "But that doesn't make me a 'slave-master'. I didn't have anything to do with all that. Maybe I am descended from slavery too, just like you! I am here to find my ancestors and find out if it's true there was a Black Jamaican in my family. "

Tony was visibly shocked, mouth open speechless, at that revelation.

"You! Black! IMPOSSIBLE!!!" Tony was irate.

"Look, I'm sorry about my breakfast suggestion." Elisabeth tried to make peace. "I am not Jamaican and I don't know everything. But I hope you will teach me what I don't know, without hating me so much."

Rupert spoke for the first time. "You couldn't have Black blood. It would show. Like me." Rupert held out his arm, brown-skinned, honey coloured. "And your hair would be like mine, not that blonde stuff." Rupert's black locks had a light, shiny curl.

"If it's true, I don't know how," said Elisabeth, "but that's what I am here to find out. I need your help and I am glad to be with you all because I think you can help me find what I am looking for."

She paused and quieted down. "So, what do you eat for breakfast? Let's find some."

There was silence for a moment, then Jacob revved up the bus, put it in gear and started again on the road. The bus drove through the western end of the capital city, navigated the crowded streets of the former capital Spanish Town past the statue in the town square of Admiral Rodney surveying his colonial domain, then flowed through the Jamaican countryside until the road ran beside a wide green river.

Just before a flat bridge that crossed the river, Jacob stopped the bus where a cluster of women were selling baskets piled with a variety of fruits.

The women rushed to the bus, pushing their baskets through each open window to offer their fruits for purchase, mangoes, naseberries, bananas, watermelon, pawpaw, jew plums, oranges, bunches of guineps, otaheiti apples. The boys made their choices, piling the fruits into a large paper bag they placed on the middle bench between Marshall and Rupert. Then it was time to pay.

"The deal was that we would drive and you would buy us food. Your plastic can't pay on the road. You have cash?" Marshall asked.

Recalling the effect her payment for gas had, Elisabeth opened her backpack and took out her wallet, opening it wide to show the thick wad of Jamaican Dollars inside. Further, as if confused, she also opened the other side of the wallet that contained an equally thick wad of English Pounds and glanced up to note all four pairs of eyes fixed on the bulky wallet in her hands. Pulling out a Ten Dollar bill, she handed it to Marshall.

"You can be the banker, Marshall. Let me know when that is finished." Snapping the wallet shut, she replaced it in her shoulder bag and leaned back in the seat, relishing the effect the sight of her money had on the men. "I'll have a banana, thank you."

Taking the money, Marshall handed it out the window,, received the change of Seven Dollars, then picked a bright gold banana from the bunch and passed it to Elisabeth. Marie poked Elisabeth gently in the side as she peeled the banana, and the two looked at each other and giggled, as the bus set off again on the road driving beside the wide river that glistened in the mid-morning sun.

The bag of fruits was dipped into frequently, as the boys ate their breakfast. Marie showed Elisabeth some of the fruits she did not know, gave her a taste of naseberry, which she did not like, and otaheiti apple which she did.

Soon they had left the riverside and were now driving through open countryside with fields and mountains, then on a narrow road winding up into the mountain. They stopped again at a wide part of the road, Jacob got out and opened the back of the bus, took out some coconuts and a machete and chopped them open.

were in Montego Bay when he came, you couldn't see him. So don't jump down the woman throat Tony. You too angry!"

Rupert intervened. "Rasta is not an easy thing to explain. You have to live it to overstand it. You can't just say what it is in a simple answer. It takes years and years to know what Rasta truly is."

"Agreed." Tony turned back to look at the road. "And a slave-master child can't understand Rasta. Only Black people can understand Rasta."

"Is Rasta only for Black people?" Marie was curious. "Was Haile Selassie Black? He looks White to me in pictures."

""No, the Emperor was not White." Rupert answered. "He was a Black Ethiopian, which is kinda like my colour, but he was an African. Ethiopia is one of the oldest African kingdoms, it goes back to the time of Egypt. The Emperor is descended from King Solomon and the Queen of Sheba."

"So you believe in a Black man as God?" Elisabeth followed up.

"Yes!" Rupert's voice was strong. "Emperor Haile Selassie is God Almighty, with NO apology." He stared at her, daring her to dispute his statement.

""It's kinda hard to believe that God is on earth today, right now, in a man in Ethiopia," Marie shook her head.

Tony turned around, took off his tam and shook his locks wildly around his head and shoulders. He pushed Rupert and Marshall aside on their seats so he could look directly at the two girls.

"Ever since the White man brought us here as slaves, they been teaching us about this White God of theirs with blue eyes and yellow hair that lives in the sky." His voice was angry. "They told us their God said that slaves should obey their massas. They told us that we were slaves because Black was ugly, was evil and God hated Black."

The word "Black" sounded like a drumbeat.

"Then one day a man named Marcus Garvey told Black people that Black was good, that the Black Man was the first man from the beginning of time and that we should love being Black."

This time the drumbeat was the slap of his stick on the back of his seat.

"He told us that Black people should only worship a God that looked like them, a Black God. Then he told us to look to Africa where a Black King would be crowned who would be our God."

Tony's tone grew less angry. "We followed the news and lo and behold, a Black man was crowned Emperor of Ethiopia, with the titles King of Kings, Lord of Lords, Conquering Lion of the Tribe of Judah, Elect of God. He was crowned by the priests of the Orthodox Church, the oldest Christian church in the world. He is a direct descendant of King Solomon and the Queen of Sheba, the two hundred and twenty-fifth to sit on the throne of Ethiopia."

"Ethiopia is where the oldest bones of man were found, just the other day. A White man found the bones of a woman, they call her 'Lucy' and she is the oldest human bones ever found. You know that Ethiopia is where the Nile starts its flow, so we can see how civilization flowed from Ethiopia to Egypt and then across the world, yes?"

Tony spread his arms.

"So these are some of the reasons why I and I Brethren are trodding the Rasta pathway right now. We kinda want to find the way to the true God, the Black God, and we find that Rasta is a perfect way to live and think as we search for that God. Rasta inspires our songs and our music."

Tony turned back in his seat to face the road and folded his arms on his chest. "I hope you overstand a little better now, both of you!"

Marie and Elisabeth looked at each other, then nodded.

"I still have more questions, though," Marie spoke to Tony's back and he waved his stick without turning.

"Save them for another conversation."

Rupert and Marshall smiled.

So they drove on in silence for several miles of narrow Jamaican road, curving and climbing over the mountain range, passing acres of red earth where the land had been mined for bauxite, then dropping through the narrow, tree-covered Fern Gully into the north coast town of Ocho Rios.

They arrived at the Ocho Rios town square, a crowded intersection of roads east and west into and out of the town, with pedestrians and cars circulating around a central island of dirt and ragged weeds that sprouted a clock tower in the center whose clock no longer worked.

Men were already at work constructing a platform over the island, others were setting up lights and massive speaker boxes, while still others stood around holding walkie-talkies which sparkled with sound when they spoke into them. Jacob pulled up the van beside a group of the walkie-talkie bearing men and Tony leaned out the window.

"Looking for Mr. Forbes. We are Whirlwind, the band."

"I am Forbes. Welcome. Sound check at 5 o'clock. You better get some lunch and find your hotel."

"Hotel? You booked us into a hotel?" Tony asked.

"You crazy?" said Mr. Thomas. "We don't book rooms for artists. Find your own hotel," and turned back to his conversation.

Jacob revved the engine and drove on.

"I guess it's the VW Hilton again tonight, guys," Rupert laughed. "I will take first turn on the back seat! HaHa Ha!!"

"Last time we went on the road, you got the back seat first!" Jacob grumbled.

"Too bad," Rupert laughed again. "I spoke first. We will give you the middle seat tonight, Fat Man."

"I will fight you if you call me 'Fat Man' again," Jacob made a first with one hand as he drove. "What about the girls?"

"Elisabeth has money for us girls to check into a hotel." Marie spoke. "I'll see if they will let us check in Marshall with us in our room, as he is my brother. Then you can park the bus in the hotel car park and sleep there tonight. Come, let's look for one."

"What kind of show is it?" Marie asked.

"It's not a show, it's a political meeting tonight," Jacob answered. "The Party is on a tour and they have hired Whirlwind Band to draw the crowds to hear them speak."

"So you belong to that Party?" Marie asked.

"Only one Party Rasta belong to," Tony spoke loudly, "that is JAH-JAH Party. Everything else is just a money gig."

They drove down the main road until they came to a big hotel, turned down a long driveway, parked at the lobby entrance. Elisabeth, Marie and Marshall got out and made their way through the clusters of American tourists smelling of sun tan oil and speaking in loud voices.

Elisabeth's white skin, English passport and credit card ensured first class attention that made check-in easy. A uniformed porter led them along corridors where the calypso music of "Yellow Bird" and "Jamaica Farewell" played on the wall speakers, to a room with two single beds and a sofa.

Marie and Elisabeth put their bags down and Elisabeth opened the glass door that led to the balcony.

Outside a wide band of golden sand edged a turquoise sea shimmering in a perfect picture of Jamaican tourism paradise. Tourists swam, paddled plastic rafts, lay on the beach browning their skin in the hot sun, or sipping drinks under beach umbrellas. It was Elisabeth's first glimpse of Jamaica's beautiful beaches and she was awestruck.

"This is so beautiful!"

She leaned over the balcony and looked out at the scene around her, at the hotel's many floors of rooms, the large swimming pool, the bars and patios where guests relaxed, the three musicians playing native instruments under a coconut tree. It all fitted perfectly her vision of Jamaica. She could see why people came to Jamaica on honeymoon. The thought of honeymoon reminded her of Michael and she frowned to remember what had caused her to set off on her Jamaican adventure. Still, it was almost worth it, to have given her a reason to see this beautiful place.

Marie had seen Jamaica's white sand beaches before, but the hotel room was a luxury she had never experienced before. Air-conditioning was a new delight and the cool air pouring into the room at a fingertip amazed her. She opened all the drawers in the dresser on which the TV set rested, found a Gideon Bible and placed it on the night table between the beds.

She flopped down on one bed that was larger than she had ever slept in before and dug her fingers into the two soft pillows that were softer than she had ever felt before. She explored the bathroom and squealed with delight to discover the small soaps, bottles of shampoo, conditioner, moisturizer and aloe vera lotion, scooping them up and putting them in her handbag. She was glad now that she had agreed to help Elisabeth. This was a nice reward already.

Marshall went back downstairs where the other band members were having an impromptu rehearsal beside the bus in a corner of the large hotel car park. Marie called room service and ordered 6 servings of toasted-cheese-and-tomato sandwiches and when they arrived, the girls packed them into a paper bag and headed out to the car park.

They ate and rested until it was time to return to the town for the band's sound check. The square was already filling up with onlookers as the band took their instruments to the back of the stage. Tony found the sound engineer, who led the band onstage to set up. Soon they were tuning Rupert's guitar and Jacob was tapping his cymbals.

Marie led Elisabeth to a spot at the side where they could see the stage and they squatted down on a low wall to wait for the event to begin. She whispered safety instructions in Elisabeth's ear: "Don't speak to anyone. Hold your shoulder bag tight. Be ready to run if I say so!"

For about an hour the sound system played some popular hit songs, while the crowd thickened. Many of them were wearing T-shirts with pictures and names of political candidates who would be speaking at the meeting.

Then Whirlwind Band took the stage. Marie and Elisabeth were surprised to see the wild reaction from the crowd as the musicians started to play and sing. Women rushed to the front of the stage shouting and waving, men jumped and waved their arms. People sang along to the choruses of their songs. Rupert's lead guitar played some beautiful melodies, while Jacko's bass set throbbing rhythms. Marshall added an African drumbeat on two Congo drums, slapping his hands on the drum-skins in rhythmic unity.

Tony strode the stage proudly, left to right like a marching army of one, a giant musical force with head held high, chest thrown back and a stern expression as he delivered lyrics that spoke of Redemption, the Victory of Good Over Evil, and the Black Revolution of Love.

By the end of their one hour set, the square was packed tight with bodies in the bright street lights that now illuminated the night. People were united by music in a celebration of happiness, unity, a glow of pure love. They cheered every song, sang along with some choruses, and screamed calling for 'MORE!' when Tony waved goodnight and led the band off the stage.

But Tony knew it was time to go, because all the politicians had come on stage and lined up behind him, ready to start their speeches, smiling and waving to the crowd as if the cheering was for them. Yes, time to leave the stage to them.

"Aren't we staying to hear the speeches?" Elisabeth asked, as Marie hurried them to meet the band as it came off stage.

Marie smiled. "For the band, listening to the speeches would be like eating bacon for breakfast."

Later, the six of them relaxed at the fishing beach on the edge of town, eating fried fish and bammy, drinking coconut water and watching the pier lights glisten on the sea. The boys brought out ganja buds and rolled them in brown paper into long cones, lit them, inhaled and gave praise in voice and in spirit to Life.

"JAH RASTAFARI" they shouted in unison, then sat meditating in ganja smoke and silence.

"You ladies want to get to Falmouth," Jacob confirmed. "Our next stop is St. Ann's Bay. We're meeting a man at Marcus Garvey's house tomorrow. As soon as we're finished, we'll head for Falmouth."

"That should be interesting," Marie was glad. "I didn't know Marcus Garvey's house was still standing.

I want to know more about that man. I know he said a lot of important things to Black people."

Marie wasn't sure she was comfortable so close to guys smoking ganja, but she knew she was supposed to act like she didn't mind. She was worried about what Elisabeth was thinking, sitting with Rastamen smoking ganja. But Elisabeth was just listening, taking it all in, smiling, not saying anything. She did speak eventually, waiting till there was a silent space in the conversation.

"I loved your music," she addressed Tony directly.

"You did? " Tony grunted. "Glad to hear."

"It made me think about good things," Elisabeth smiled.

There was silence.

"Did you hear when I sang that White people mus' pay for slavery?"

There was silence again.

"Yes, I heard that part too. That made me think also."

"Well think about it some more." Tony got up and walked away further down the beach and lit his spliff again, blowing the smoke up into the sky.

There was another long silence.

"Don't mind Tony." It was Rupert, trying to make light of the moment. "Glad you like the Whirlwind band. That was just a little of our music. We have lots more. We love music. We are music. We want everyone to love our music."

"Well, I hope to hear more." Elisabeth smiled, determined not to let Tony see she was hurt by his response. "It's time to take us back to the hotel. Is Jacob ready?"

CHAPTER TWENTY

MARCUS GARVEY

Elisabeth woke early, put on her swimsuit and a robe and went down to the beach. There were few swimmers in the sea and she dived in with a feeling of freedom. The water was warm and clear, so pure blue it was like a bright clear tunnel that could take her straight around the world. She surfaced, lay on her back, then turned and swam parallel to the beach for a short distance.

She dived again under water, then surfaced and floated on her back looking up at the blue and gold skies above her. Yes, Jamaica was beautiful.

Coming out of the water, Elisabeth lay down on a beach chair and rested. She was surprised to hear a "Hello" from close by and turned to see Marshall also stretched out on a beach chair.

"I decided to give you girls your privacy in the room, so I slept here last night." He waved a wrist on which he wore a coloured plastic band identifying him as a hotel guest.

"Security tried to throw me out, but I just showed them my band," he smiled. "I'll come up and take a shower, though."

They returned to the room, where Marie was still in bed trying hard not to get out of it. She had enjoyed the night sleeping in that soft bed with its crisp sheet and soothing blanket under the cool air-conditioning. But even nicer than the bed would be breakfast in the big hotel dining room.

Soon all three were dressed, packed and downstairs, helping themselves from the wide selection of food on the hotel's breakfast buffet stations. Breakfast over, Marshall filled a napkin with an assortment of breads, muffins and biscuits and took them to the bus while Elisabeth checked out of the hotel.

Packing up the bus again, they set off, first stopping outside Ocho Rios at a Rasta village of small dwellings camped on both sides of a natural stream that ran through the land. There amid water hyacinths, ducklings, small children and hummingbirds drinking from hibiscus flowers, Tony, Jacob and Rupert took a bath in the river and sat for a while speaking and smoking with some Rastamen with long dreadlocks. Then it was back on the road to St. Ann's Bay and Marcus Garvey's house.

St. Ann's Bay was a small, untidy town of narrow streets overhung by two storey buildings made of wood in Jamaican style, and a few concrete structures housing merchants, banks and building societies. The roads north to south ran up and down a steep hillside and it was on one of these the bus came to a stop before a ramshackle house that looked in danger of falling down.

The wood was gray with age and rotting in several places. The stone steps leading up the small hill on which it was set, were broken. The roof was rusty zinc.

"THIS is the home of your first National Hero!" Elisabeth was shocked. "I don't believe it!"

"I agree!" Marie was stunned. "This is terrible! I am ashamed to see this, as a Jamaican! How come?"

"Like the song says, 'No one remembers old Marcus Garvey'." Rupert sang the line from a song that was popular on the radio. "People say Garvey talks about race too much, makes people remember slavery, tells people they should go back to Africa. Some people don't like to hear things like that so they kinda keep Garvey hidden. They don't really care about Africa and being Black. They want us to remain colonials, loving England and English culture that we inherited from the time of slavery.

"But how stupid it is to think like that. They don't see that it's time for us to let go of that thinking and get back to thinking the African way, like the people we were before they brought us here, African people. So that is why we sing our songs, to teach them a different way of thinking, knowing we are Black, African people."

"So why exactly are we here?" Marie asked.

"We are here to pay tribute to the spirit of Mr. Garvey and to take some photos for the cover of the first Whirlwind Band album in front of the home of the man who said '*Look for me in the whirlwind*'!"

Marie and Elisabeth looked puzzled.

" You don't know anything about Marcus Garvey, do you? You don't know he said that when he was gone we should look for him to return in the whirlwind and thunder?" Rupert asked. The girls shook their heads.

"He did. We named our band after Mr. Garvey's prophesy because we want people to hear Mr. Garvey's whirlwind in our songs." Tony added his voice.

"We teach his message in our songs telling Black people to 'emancipate themselves from mental slavery'. We tell Black people to look to Africa and build it up great again, like it used to be before slavery, before the White man took us from Africa and took our continent from us. That was the message of Marcus Garvey that we bring in the Whirlwind!"

A small car drove up and a young man jumped out, apologizing for being late and immediately directing the band members where to stand and how to pose, before taking several photos on the steps and verandah of the little broken-down house.

"We're gonna fix up this place one day soon," he kept saying, as he moved swiftly taking his photos.

"The Parish Council promises to build Mr. Garvey a statue at the Library, and we are still hoping the Government will allocate some funds to repair the house. All we get is 'Soon come'. Just have to keep trying."

"You go-on wait for them people," Tony thundered. "When Whirlwind album make Number One, we will rebuild the place in Mr. Garvey's memory.'

"For real!" Three voices echoed, as they joined hands together in a Black Power salute.

The photographer stopped, looked at them all, then realized he had just missed capturing the best moment, begged them "Do that again!" But the boys just laughed and tumbled down off the steps, got into the van, followed by the girls, and drove off out of St. Ann's Bay along the coast road beside the sea towards Falmouth.

"So tell me some more about Marcus Garvey," Elisabeth spoke in the silence. "He must have said a lot for them to make him a National Hero, but it seems they didn't like him much, if this is how they honour him!"

Tony answered. "The best thing he said was that Black people should stop worshiping a White god. He said:

'If the White man has the idea of a White God, let him worship his God as he desires. If the yellow man's God is of his race let him worship his God as he sees fit. We, as Negroes, have found a new ideal. Whilst our God has no color, yet since the white people have seen their God through White spectacles, we have only now started out to see our God through our own spectacles. The God of Isaac and the God of Jacob let Him exist for the race that believes in the God of Isaac and the God of Jacob. We Negroes believe in the God of Ethiopia'"

Tony smiled as the others looked at him with wide open eyes. "I had to learn that speech for a school fete when I was 12 and I never forgot it. The teacher said I was the only student Black enough to play Garvey. I was so vex when he said that, 'cause I didn't know anything about Africa and I hated being called 'Black enough', but now I am glad."

"Tony told you it was Mr. Garvey who said we must look to Africa for the crowning of a Black King, and then when His Majesty was crowned Emperor of Ethiopia and it was clearly fulfillment of prophecy, so you can see why Rasta think of Garvey as a Prophet, kind of like John the Baptist," Jacob added.

"What did he say about the 'whirlwind'?" Marie asked. Tony was glad to speak the words. He held up one arm in an oratorical pose.

"When I am dead wrap the mantle of the Red, Black and Green around me, for in the new life I shall rise with God's grace and blessing to lead the millions up the heights of triumph with the colors that you well know. Look for me in the whirlwind or the storm, look for me all around you, for, with God's grace, I shall come and bring with me countless millions of black slaves who have died in America and the West Indies and the millions in Africa to aid you in the fight for Liberty, Freedom and Life."

"RASTAFARI!!!" Four voices shouted the Rasta clarion call, echoed by "Selassie I!!!"

Silence filled the bus again as they travelled, giving Elisabeth time to think about the conversations and experiences she was having in the company of these young and Black Jamaicans.

Slavery ... race ... poverty ... Black ... Africa ... these were not words she heard expressed or talked about at any time of her growth and life. She had enjoyed concerts by Black singers like Aretha Franklin and The Supremes at the Albert Hall, just as much as she enjoyed concerts by Janis Joplin and the Rolling Stones.

But she had never considered racial matters, or taken a moment to consider the life of the Black people she passed on London streets. She knew she was not prejudiced against Black people because she was great friends with the pretty brown-skinned girl who worked at her favourite Kings Road boutique where she shopped on weekends, and she received great service from the Indian take-away restaurant in Notting Hill Gate that she visited often.

But this was her first confrontation with the role people of her colour, race and nationality had played in the lives and countries of people of another race, colour and nationality like those she was traveling with. It made her a little frightened, especially when she saw the hatred and disgust Tony had for her. She could separate that hatred from herself personally, as she could see the others were not as bitter, but she realized she had to face up to what people like her had done to create such hatred and bitterness.

It gave her a lot to think about, as she searched for the possibility of a trace of Black blood in her family and her life. What if she should find a Black ancestor? Would that change her? And if so, how? Would she now be considered a victim instead of a victor? Would she be loved now, not hated? The answers to those questions made the search even more important for Elisabeth.

CHAPTER TWENTYONE

FALMOUTH -THE SEARCH

The town of Falmouth sits on a wide harbour on the north-western side of Jamaica. For centuries it was one of the chief ports to which Africans were unloaded off ships from the African Continent and sold in slave auctions. English ships captains who had supervised the brutality of the Middle Passage, unloaded their brutal cargo at Falmouth pier. Jewish merchants handled the buying and selling of the trade, as well as the shipment of merchandise necessary to conduct the business and work of slavery, from offices in buildings designed to reflect typical 18th Century English architecture.

Much had been done to preserve the remnants of the historic buildings of slavery days, and the market in the town square was fenced by a beautiful wrought-iron grill that advertised its slave history

with a sign giving details. The preparations for the
upcoming public meeting were already evident,
scaffolding, speaker boxes and lights being unloaded
from a truck. Jacob brought the bus to a stop outside
one of the old buildings over whose door was a sign
"Trelawny Parish Council".

"This is where you will find records. You have
to ask someone inside here," said Jacob. "Our sound
check is right here at 5. There's a nice beach outside
the town. We're going to chill out there and eat some
fish, before the check. Marshall will come find you
when it's time."

Marie and Elisabeth got out of the bus and
went into the building. A Receptionist directed them
to Miss Edwards, the Librarian, a gray-haired lady
wearing thick spectacles who surveyed them with
curiosity and a smile. Marie smiled back. "Hello. We
are doing some research for some studies we are
doing at UWI and want to find some information."

"What information? What years specifically?
About slavery, I bet." Miss Edwards smile widened.

"Yes," Marie admitted. "We are looking for
some records for sales of slaves between the years

1750 to 1780. Did the Parish keep records of those transactions?"

"That's a tall order," Miss Edwards looked over her glasses. "Yes, there are boxes and boxes of ledgers in the basement vault," she admitted. "There's a lot to look through. Government keeps promising to build a library to preserve them, because there is no space at the Institute of Jamaica in Kingston."

Marie and Elisabeth looked at each other with happy eagerness.

"We would be glad to look through them. We're here till tomorrow."

Miss Edwards led them through narrow corridors and down a flight of stairs to the basement. It smelled musty and insects scuttled out of the way as the door opened. On the walls were shelves and shelves of hundreds of thick leather-bound ledgers, their dates painted white on the spine. Miss Edwards spread her arms.

"See what I mean?"

The girls' shoulders drooped. Elisabeth sighed, but the memory of her mission strengthened her.

"It's OK." She slung her shoulder bag on a table in the center of the room, took out a bottle of water and sat down on a chair. "Show us where to begin."

To Marie she said: "We're looking for a ship's captain named Grant and a slave named Mercy. Let's start looking for our needle in this haystack."

The noise in the town square of the sound check, the Whirlwind Band performance and the several political speeches of the night blasted through the loudspeakers and kept Marie and Elisabeth company in the basement all night, as they leafed through volume after volume of records of slaves bought and sold, their names, ages, conditions, sale price, ship of origin, captain's name, ship's registry and country.

Other ledgers contained lists of slave transactions between owners in Falmouth and plantations in the other Parishes. They worked all night turning page after page, till they heard Marshall banging on the basement door, accompanied by the Parish Council security guard who knew they were working inside.

"I want us to find three rooms tonight and get a good rest," Elisabeth announced when they got into the bus. "This looks like a town where we can find a clean guest house."

"Thank you. That's very kind of you Elisabeth," said Rupert. "I know one I stayed at one time. Drive down this street Jacko."

"I don't need no room. I will sleep in the bus," Tony folded his arms on his chest. "More room to stretch out now without you guys snoring in my ears all night. Sleep tight in you' sof' beds!"

Elisabeth could take no more.

"You know, you could be handsome if you weren't so angry all the time!" She laughed sweetly. "A smile might be a pretty sight!"

Everyone joined in the laughter, except Tony who pulled his tam down over his head and scrunched down in the seat. The laughter still filled the bus as they found a cosy guest house in the back streets of Falmouth with three clean, tidy rooms, a bathroom with hot water and a promise of steamed callaloo and bammy for breakfast in the morning from a plump country woman happy to have paying guests.

The sound of rain on the roof was comforting as morning dawned. Breakfast was waiting on a small table in the lobby as Marie and Elisabeth left the men sleeping in their rooms and waited for a break in the showers to walk back to the Parish Council building and continue their search in the basement ledgers.

"This will take forever," Marie sighed at lunchtime. "We will be here for days!"

Elisabeth sighed too.

There was a tap on the door and Miss Edwards opened it and came in. "How is it going, girls?"

"Not very well, Miss Edwards," Elisabeth sighed. "Seems endless."

"What exactly are you looking for?" Miss Edward sat down.

"We are trying to find a ship's captain who we think took a slave woman back to England with him."

"That happened all the time," Miss Edwards. "Male and female slaves were taken, but there are special records for that as permission had to be given, because once the slave arrived in England he or she would be automatically free." She got up and walked to a section of the shelves and took out two volumes.

"Look in these. Was it a man or a woman?"

"A woman. More than that, she could have been a white-skinned slave!"

"Then that shouldn't be hard to find in this book. She would have been listed as 'mulatto' or 'quadroon' or 'octoroon'. You can just look for those entries."

"Wow! Thank you so MUCH Miss Edwards! You have helped us so much!" Elisabeth threw her arms around Miss Edwards, almost knocking her glasses off with the happy embrace.

"You should have told me,' Miss Edwards smiled. "It would have saved you a a lot of time. Happy hunting."

Marie and Elisabeth turned to the new pile of ledgers. There was still a lot of searching to be done, but this time it was easier. Success came two hours later.

"Here it is!" Marie pointed to the line in the ledger:

"1765: Sold, Mercy, octoroon female house slave 17 years, property of Charles Ratcliffe, Maryville estate, St.Mary. Sold to Merchant ship Captain James Grant, Thirty-Five Pounds."

Elisabeth let out a whoop of joy.   Marie heaved a sigh of relief.

"Thank God. At last we know." Marie smiled with happiness.

"Come, let me take a picture of this page. Best way to copy it." Elisabeth took out her camera, fixed on a flashbulb and clicked several times.

"It's over now, isn't it?" Marie was happy. "We've found the lady in the painting, the White/Black slave lady in your family." She spoke optimistically. "We can just stay with the boys now and enjoy their show in Montego Bay, yes?"

"No, we still don't know who she was, where she came from and how they met." Elisabeth was serious. "We still have to find her. I have to find the plantation she came from, find out who her father and mother were. It's not over yet."

"The boys were planning to drive to MoBay and spend tonight at a friend's house, have a little holiday. The show is not till tomorrow night," Marie explained as they took a taxi from the Parish Council building back to the guest house. The rain was still falling, heavier now and small rivers ran in the street-side gutters, while dark overhead skies promised even heavier rain to come.

Marie was hoping to have some holiday time too. To tell the truth, she wanted to get to know Tony better. She was attracted to Tony's rebel spirit and his anger at the history of his people. She wanted to know more of his knowledge about Black history, the Bible, righteousness.

Yes, he could be handsome, as Elisabeth had said. She remembered how he looked on stage, head held high, chest thrown back, strong legs marching across the stage like an African warrior, his beautiful voice singing songs of freedom. She wondered if he had a girlfriend. She wondered what being his girlfriend would be like. She wouldn't mind having some time to relax and get to know him away from the stress of performing and the equal stress for him of Elisabeth's company.

"We still don't know who Mercy was and how she came to be White or to be going to England with the first Captain Grant. I need to go to St. Mary and find the plantation she came from," Elisabeth explained.

"I don't know how we're going to work it out with the band. We're going to have to wait till they do their show in Montego Bay, then this job will be finished and they can concentrate on helping us find Mercy. I realize we just MUST find out who she was." Marie agreed reluctantly.

CHAPTER TWENTYTWO

MONTEGO BAY

The rain was coming down stronger, as the bus set off for Montego Bay. The wipers swished loudly across the windshield, pushing away thick splashes of water, clearing a double triangle view of the road through the thick rain that made visibility difficult. In some places the road was completely covered in water, hiding deep potholes into which the bus occasionally fell. They drove on through the rainstorm, wish flashes of lightning occasionally brightening the gloom.

"How much longer to MoBay?" Marie asked.

"We should be there in another hour, just get there before dark." Jacob answered.

Just then the bus dropped with a loud thud into a large pool of water that hid a hole in the road and it stopped, the engine still running.

"RAAAS" Jacob shouted the familiar Jamaican expletive. He turned off the engine. "I bet we have a flat now." he slapped the steering wheel. "Come guys, let's get out and push."

The four got out and with several heaves, pushed the bus out of the hole and over to the side of the road. The front left tire was flat. Set back from the road was a small shop under whose verandah roof a few people sheltered from the downpour. The four went over to them.

"Anyone fix tire around here?" Jacob asked one of the men sheltering.

"No, sah. You going have to reach MoBay to fix that," the man answered. "You have a spare? Push the bus down here and we will help you put on the spare."

"We have a spare, but it's smooth," Jacob shrugged. "We have to use it though."

The men pushed the bus closer to the shop, Marie and Elisabeth got out and went inside the little shop entrance to wait and watch, while the men helped jack up the vehicle and change the tire.

"This is rapidly becoming the journey from hell," Elisabeth pouted. "Where did all this rain come from?"

"Just be glad we found shelter." Marie was stoic. "It could have happened in the middle of nowhere."

"I thought THIS was the middle of nowhere," Elisabeth was still upset.

It took about half an hour and much angry swearing for the bus to be relieved of one tire and fitted with another. The jack stood in inches of water while Jacob, Tony and Rupert took turns cranking the handle up to raise the vehicle off the ground, then unscrew the lug nuts, take off the busted tire and put on the spare. By the time the bus was jacked back down and the tools stored in the back, they all were soaking wet.

Inside the shop Elisabeth gave Marshall money to buy cold beers, sodas, packs of crackers and slices of cheese which they drank and ate on the pavement outside, watching the rain pelt down with looks of disappointment on everyone's faces. Then with a heaving sigh, Tony said: "Time to get back on the road. We have to reach MoBay before night."

"Best place to fix that tire in the rain will be the gas station at the airport," the man who helped them said as they got back into the bus. "Nowhere else will be open in this storm."

Back inside the bus, they pulled towels and dry shirts out of the bundle of bags in the clutter at the back, squeezed water out of their socks and put on their wet shoes again. The bus was hot and steamy, smelling of sweaty bodies and musty shoes, as they drove on to Montego Bay.

Rivers of water rushed down both sides of the road and flowed over into the middle, as the bus seemed to surf through the flooded road. Outside they could see the sea on the right of the road, churning rolls of brown water crashing with foamy white surf onto the beach. Few cars passed them, only a big truck that made a splash that almost flooded the bus engine.

The flat lands of the Montego Bay airport came into view, empty runways with small and larger planes sitting silently, waiting for the storm to ebb.

Jacob turned down the road and drove to the entrance of the Departure Lounge. A porter rushed up to greet the bus with an umbrella and a trolley, expecting departing visitors. Jacob asked and got directions to the small gas station that could be seen at one end of the compound where some taxis were parked awaiting customers.

"Leave us here," Elisabeth opened the bus door and reached for her bag. "There must be a bathroom here where we can dry off and find some real food." She and Marie got out, followed by Marshall, determined not to leave them alone – especially if food was on the agenda.

Inside they found a Ladies room, used the toilet and put on dry clothes. Then they looked around the lobby for a restaurant and found a cafe offering hamburgers, milk shakes and plastic-wrapped cheese & tomato sandwiches. They ordered six sandwiches, three milk shakes and waited for the rest of the band to join them with a report on the bus tire.

"They can repair the tire but not till tomorrow morning," Jacob gave the report. "We're going to have to take a taxi into town tonight to find the friend we are staying with. You girls can take another taxi to find a hotel. Looks like this is the end of the road for now."

"Oh no, this is terrible. I need to get back on the road." Elisabeth was not pleased. "I really need to go in the opposite direction, not go into Montego Bay. It's awful that we just have to wait here in this rain for another day and night. I need to get to St. Mary. No taxi is going to want to go on the road in this rain. I wish I could fly!"

There was a loud laugh from a man who had been sitting at a corner table in the cafe, reading a newspaper. "You wish you could fly! That's so funny." He folded up his paper, got up and came over to their table.

"What is so funny?" Tony took charge of the group, standing to face the man as he approached. He was tall, slim and brown-skinned, graying a little at the temples and in the short beard he sported. He wore a white shirt and khaki trousers.

The man held up his arms in a gesture of surrender, still smiling. "Peace, my brother, Peace. I am laughing because I heard the young lady say she wished she could fly. Flying is what I do. I fly planes," he laughed again. "Where do you want to go, my lady?" He bowed.

Elisabeth smiled. "I haven't missed my flight. I'm only trying to get to St. Mary, not back to England. You're a jet pilot?"

"No, no, no. And I am just waiting for the rain to ease up so I can fly my little plane back to St. Mary. I overheard you talking. Can I sit down?"

Elisabeth was immediately interested. "Of course, sit down. Your little plane? You have a plane that can fly? You mean you could fly me to St. Mary?" The words poured out of her.

"Yes," the man said. "I am Tony Bradshaw. I fly crop duster planes. I left Tinson Pen airport in Kingston this morning to do a job, but the rain has made it impossible to do any work. I had to land here and wait out the storm. But I have to get back by tomorrow. If my weather senses are still functioning, the rain is going to ease up early morning. I am sure if I get an early start I can get back before it comes down again. If you're feeling adventurous, there's an airstrip in Portland I could drop you off at on my way back home."

Elisabeth thought about this. "Are you serious?" She looked at Marie, and at the boys. "What do you think? Would you come with me Marie?"

Marie was shocked. "Fly? I've never flown in a plane. Sounds crazy to me."

But Marshall leaned over. "I would do it. I would love to fly in a plane. Like bird. Whoosh!" He stretched out his arms like wings and flapped them with a laugh.

"Who asked you?" Marie pushed her brother.

"Mama said I wasn't to leave you two alone, so I have to come wherever you go." He sat down.

Elisabeth turned to Tony. "What do you say, Tony? Would you mind if we left you here? We could meet up again after you finish in Montego Bay. The bus will be fixed and you can come for us in St. Mary."

Tony shrugged. "I don't care. If you want to put your life in this man's hands, go ahead. But only birds fly."

"To tell the truth," Bradshaw said. "I've heard old people say that one time long ago the people could fly!"

"I don't believe that," Tony was still in charge.

Elisabeth turned to the man Bradshaw. "Will it be safe? I've flown a lot. I am not afraid, but can you take the three of us?"

"It will be a squeeze, but yes, there's space. Only thing is you would have to stay out here with me tonight because as soon as there is light in the morning and the rain has eased up, I will be heading out."

"How long will the trip take?"

"About 20 minutes, half an hour, not long. The island is small."

"Well it's done then." Elisabeth stood up. "Marshall, please help me get our bags out of the bus."

Tony stood up and walked over to where Marie sat. "Are you sure you want to do this Marie?"

Marie was surprised, and pleased at Tony's concern. "I'm kinda scared, but I can't leave her. I am committed. She's family." She looked up at him.

He was silent. Marshall got up and so did Rupert.

"You wait here Elisabeth," Rupert stretched out a hand to stop her. "I will go with him to get the bags. I'm not going to leave you here alone. We all are going to wait here with you till this man's plane takes off, whenever it goes."

"We might as well," said Jacob, "cause the bus can't drive any more tonight in this rain with no spare. I will stay with the bus." Jacob picked up the keys and the two of them headed out to the bus. Tony sat down beside Marie.

"Let me buy you a beer, Ras," said Mr. Bradshaw to Tony. "And a cup of tea for you, milady?" He made a mock bow to Elisabeth with a smile, "It's going to be a long night."

It was indeed a long night. Elisabeth spent most of it telling Bradshaw about coming to Jamaica to search for her ancestor and what they had found so far. He told her stories about Jamaican slavery that were simple facts, not criticisms, that helped her see a broader picture of Jamaican history and of how slavery worked as an economic institution for producing sugar.

"Sugar was the richest product in Europe at the time and the sugar plantations were the factories producing that wealth by using human labour as production machines. One man named Beckford had 700 plantations? He was so rich, he used his wealth to build a high tower on his estate in England, but the cost bankrupted him."

"Served him right!" Elisabeth laughed.

"A lot of the plantations like his went bankrupt when slavery was abolished. Some of the owners just left their slaves to starve and went home to England, leaving the estates in ruin. Some of them stayed, bought more land and brought in indentured servants from India to farm the cane, but most of the estates just crumbled into ruins. You can see some of the old great-house ruins from the air, sugar mills, factory walls, all broken down, covered with plants and weeds."

"You know a lot about Jamaica," Marie admitted. "They don't teach us those stories at school. They only teach us that Jamaica started with slavery."

"The details are too ugly to tell children, that's probably why they don't teach about slavery in school" Bradshaw lit another cigarette.

"You're looking for a St. Mary plantation?" he asked. Elisabeth nodded. "A lot of the slaves on the St. Mary plantations were runaways they captured in the Maroon wars."

"Tell us about those wars."

"The English didn't give up without a fight when their slaves started running away to be free, you know. They waged war on them. Slaves were valuable possessions, they couldn't just allow them to run away. There were three Maroon wars. They fought them in Trelawny, in the Cockpit Country where most of today's Maroons still live.

But the most bitter Maroon wars were fought in the east, in the Blue Mountains where the largest group of Maroons lived at a place called Nanny Town in Portland. They had a woman as their general and they say she was a badder warrior than even the men."

"I've heard about her," Marie spoke. "That was the woman they call Nanny."

"Yes, that was Nanny the woman warrior." Bradshaw continued. 'I don't mean to be rude, but they have a legend about her that she used to catch bullets in her backside and fire them back at the English soldiers."

The girls giggled. "For real! Some woman warrior," Elisabeth laughed.

"Well, after the Third Maroon war, they English captured a lot of runaways at Nanny Town and to make sure they didn't join up again, they sold them far away from each other. Some went to St. Mary, some to St. Ann and some as far as Trelawny. The lady you're looking for could have been sent to any of those estates. You're looking for a needle in a haystack. Your great, great grand-lady, she was one of the lucky ones. She got away. "

"So what should I do to find her?" Elisabeth asked.

"If I was you, I would go up to Cornwall Barracks in the Portland where Nanny Town used to be. There is a Maroon community still there and the Colonel could tell you a lot of history. They hand down their oral history and can tell you things going back several generations," Bradshaw explained.

"How can we get there from the airport when we land?

"I can phone a man with a Land Rover to meet us when we land and drive you there. The road is bad and you can't find your way by yourself. But seriously, that's where I would look first."

"Thank you, you've been a great help," Elisabeth was content. "I want to pay you for the flight. How much?"

"Look, the gas has already been paid for by the farmer whose crop I was to spray, and he's going to have to pay me again to do it when the rain stops, so just let this be a little show of Jamaican hospitality," Bradshaw smiled. "It's not often I get to fly some pretty ladies. It's usually just fat farmers smelling of manure. Let me go and make that phone call. Soon come."

"Thank you very much," Elisabeth stretched out her to shake and Bradshaw shook it with a smile.

Rupert stood up. "Come with me, Elisabeth. I've put some chairs together over here for you and Marie to stretch out on. Come, try and get some rest."

The chairs were uncomfortable, designed to discourage any travelers unfortunate enough to be waiting in the airport lobby at night from falling asleep, but they had to suffice.

Marshall rested his head on a table and slept.

Bradshaw smoked cigarettes and listened to the rain falling.

Marie found that Tony was sitting right beside her line of chairs, so she got her chance to speak with him in soft whispers about Garvey and history and Blackness and to ask him what Love meant to a Rasta.

And Rupert got a chance to ask Elisabeth all about life in England, what the music scene was like, what countries she had visited and what were the things that made her happy.

CHAPTER TWENTYTHREE
PORTLAND

It seemed like only a short while later that day dawned light enough to see outside. Marshall was the only one sleeping and Bradshaw's "Everybody up!" was enough to rouse them all. Marie, Elisabeth and Marshall picked up their bags, said goodbye to Tony and Rupert and followed Bradshaw outside.

On the rain wet runway, giant jets stood perched high on their massive wheels waiting to accept passengers. Bradshaw strode to a far corner of the tarmac where small planes were parked and headed to the smallest one. He, Marie, Elisabeth and Marshall climbed into the plane and strapped themselves into the small seats with their bags clutched to their chests.

Bradshaw revved the engine and taxied the plane to the tarmac, drove it down the take-off strip and suddenly they were airborne. Marie caught her breath as she felt her stomach drop. She was scared. It was bad enough to be flying in such a small and flimsy looking plane, but the dark skies above made the flight seem even more dangerous.

Below them Jamaica's green was visible occasionally through rising mist and low clouds, as the plane flew on over the mountain peaks below. Once she looked down and saw a river like a brown ribbon cutting across the waterlogged land and she could see where it flowed into the sea, turning it brown.

Sometimes they seemed to fly too close to the mountains, almost if she could reach down and touch the tops. Looking down made Marie shiver. She held her breath, closed her eyes and prayed, holding Marshall's hand as tightly as he held hers.

Elisabeth had flown many times, in large and small planes over snow-covered mountains, African deserts and in private jets to visit rich European friends. This trip was only memorable for her because of the surprising way it had come about – a miracle, was the only way she could think about it. The noise of the engine gave her time to think back over the past few days since she came to Jamaica. She reached into her bag, took out her notebook and stared at the face of the woman in the painting.

"Lady Mercy", she spoke in her mind. "You sent me on this mission, didn't you? It's *you* who wants me to find you."

The face framed by blonde curls stared back at her. Was that a small smile at the corner of the woman's mouth? Elisabeth sighed. It was out of her hands now. She had to simply relax and let it all flow till it reached the end.

The rain started falling, light drops hitting the wings and splashing sideways on the plastic windows. The plane's engine sputtered as Bradshaw changed gears for the descent.

"Hang on!" he shouted over his shoulder, as the little plane rocked and fell on the updrafts. The wings tilted up to the left, then to the right, then straightened up with the nose pointed down. Barely visible in front was a small airstrip that looked more like a straight piece of Jamaica's narrow highway, hardly long enough to hold a car let alone land an airplane.

Marie closed her eyes again, held her breath and prayed. She dared not look.

Then there was a big bump, a bang and another two bumps, and she realized they had landed. Bradshaw applied the brakes and the plane slid to a bumpy stop just as the runway ran out.

"Not bad, eh?" Bradshaw smiled as he taxied the plane to a small covered shed where a few men stood beside some vehicles. Getting out of the plane, he led Marie, Elisabeth and Marshall to greet the people who waited under shelter of the building.

"Elisabeth, this is Mr. Parry," Bradshaw introduced them. "He farms coffee up in the Blue Mountains. He says he will drive you up to Maroon country,"

Mr. Parry was short and stocky with a big belly. He smiled and stepped forward to greet them. 'You look like my niece," he said when he shook Marie's hand.

Bradshaw stretched out a hand saying goodbye to Marshall, and then embraced both girls, an arm around each and planted a kiss on each girl's cheek.

"I'm off again, gotta try and get to Kingston before this rain falls any harder. You ladies have my card. I'd love to know if you ever find your Mercy, Elisabeth. It would be a good story to add to my collection."

And slapping his hat on his head, he ran to the plane whose engine was still running, taxied the plane through the rain to the end of the runway, turned it around and in a minute was in the air again, heading over the mountains to Kingston.

*   *   *   *   *

The route selected to find the free blacks of the mountains was one from St. George parish, by way of the estate of Colonel Hobby, which was located in the valley of the Swift River. ... On May 30 they started the hike into the interior, marching south-easterly and crossing Foxe's River several times. Nightfall found them on a high mountain ridge where they pitched camp.

The following day they continued to march south-easterly, crossing several smaller rivers, camping again overnight on the side of one of these. At this time they were near some Maroon settlements and at daybreak on June 1 they entered a deserted Maroon town. Here the baggage bearers helped themselves to Maroon food crops which were used to replenish their stocks of food. They destroyed the remainder of the cultivations sof bananas and plantains before they left.

They then followed a path uphill, alongside a river which flowed at the foot of the Blue Mountains. After marching for two days and two nights, resting as they found it necessary, they were on a high ridge of the Blue Mountains, just above the village of Nanny Town. From this position, a short climb took them to the Grand Ridge, where they followed a Maroon pathway along the ridge for another two days.

On June 6 they found themselves looking down into a valley where a large Maroon plantation was located. It was south-east of where they were and they thought that they could reach it after another day's marching. That objective was achieved by midday on the 7th.

Plysham told the Council, before which he appeared some time later, that the Maroon town was well developed. When they had finally reached the plantations, they saw good roads leading up into the mountain and they thought that this was possibly a road for the purpose of bringing down timber. Marching further, they observed Maroon people working in the fields, planting and weeding their crops. Further view was obstructed by the vegetation and so Soaper climbed a tree to obtain a better view and found that from that position he could look into the town which was established in a valley beside a river. Soaper took a decision to wait until daybreak the following day before entering the town. However, by doing this, they transferred the advantage to the Maroon warriors.

Of course, the Maroons had by then realized that they were about to be attacked. This was patently obvious when the militia next reconnoitred the town from the position at the top of the tree. Their greatest fears were realized when they saw about 100 women running up a broad road across the mountain carrying bundles of their possessions and their children following behind them. There was at this point nothing further to be gained by delaying their entry, and so Soaper ordered a detachment of his men to march towards the tow, which they found to be below a precipice.

In the town the Maroons were hurriedly implementing the military plan developed for such occasions. Personal and household possessions, consisting of pots, plates, utensils, musical instruments and clothing, were quickly gathered into cloth bundles. They evacuated the town, to take cover in established outcamps and other villages higher up the mountain and out of reach of gunfire. The warriors armed themselves with muskets and cutlasses and took up a defensive position in the bush which surrounded the town. There they waited.

In the morning Soaper sent an advance party of twenty down the precipice into the town. When they were fired upon, Suaper ordered them to retreat. But by this time the soldiers were within the safu ground (military meeting place or dancing ground) and were surrounded by the Maroons who engaged them in close fighting, wiping out most of the advance party.[7]

*   *   *   *

Mr. Parry's stomach barely fit under the steering wheel of the mud-covered Land Rover as he drove the country road towards Port Antonio. The rain was falling more thickly now, but the Land Rover didn't mind either the potholes or the water, driving along like a tank with strong wipers clearing the windshield. They drove past large acres of coconut trees on one side of the road swaying in the weight of the rain on another stretch of road groves of banana trees drooped under water-flooded fields.

The vehicle drove through small towns where the collection of small houses on either side of the highway

---

[7]   THE MAROON STORY: The Authentic and Original History of the Maroons in the History of Jamaica 1490-1880: Bev Carey; A Descendant of the 'first time' Maroons' Agouti Press 1997 P. 197

ended as quickly as they began. At one point the road ran beside the sea, a roaring monster whose waves surged brown and white and fell angrily on the black sands. Soon they had driven down the hill overlooking Navy Island into Port Antonio, turning right at the town square and up through the town on the road to Fellowship.

After driving through the small town of Berrydale, they came to a crossing where one sign pointed to "Rafting on the Rio Grande" and another said "Cornwall Barracks".

Mr. Parry put the Land Rover in 4-wheel drive and spoke for the first time to his passengers. "We going into the Maroon's lands, so we going to ask permission of the spirits."

He reached across Marshal sitting in the front seat, opened the glove compartment and took out a small flask of white rum. Rolling down the window on his side, Parry opened the flask, took a swig of the rum and sprayed it from his mouth out of the window. Then he spoke some words that could not be understood, capped the bottle and replaced it safely.

Seeing that his passengers were surprised, he explained further "Maroons keep company with plenty spirits. Don't want to make the spirits angry that we come into their place without permission," he smiled and started the car up the road.

"Did he say 'spirits'?" Marie whispered to Elisabeth, sitting in the back seat beside her. Elisabeth just opened her eyes wide.

Now they were driving into true mountain country. A river ran through large gray rocks in the valley beside them on the right hand. At times the road dipped down level with the river, or at times high on the hillside overlooking the rushing water made brown by the rain. Water grasses lined the riversides, wild ginger plants bloomed red spears, bamboo plumes floated high in feathery bunches on the hillsides. This was country accustomed to rain. The plants were enjoying the pelting bath like children playing in the rain. Flowers filled deep throats with the precious water and the river's rustle and crackle showed it joy at being filled full with its favourite child – the rainstorm.

They drove through Comfort Castle, Millbank and over Alligator Church Bridge, past little houses that looked no different from other little Jamaican houses, but whose inhabitants looked at the passing vehicle with the look of disdain given to uninvited visitors.

Finally a sign said Cornwall Barracks. Mr. Parry stopped his vehicle in front of a shop where a few people stood looking at the rain falling heavily and splashing into the puddles.

"We looking for the Colonel," Mr. Parry put his head out the window.

"Colonel Wood up at the School House," a man pointed to a white-painted concrete block building nearby surrounded by neatly manicured lawn, a hibiscus hedge and large otaheiti apple trees bursting with bright red fruits. In the yard beside the house were two small circular thatch-roofed huts made of sticks stuck into the ground, then interwoven with other sticks and vines to make walls. Mr. Parry drove the Land Rover up to the house and got out.

A man carrying a large black umbrella came out of the house and down the steps to the vehicle. Mr. Parry met him under the umbrella, spoke a few words to him and gestured towards the people waiting in the vehicle. Then he beckoned to them to come out. Marie, Elisabeth and Marshall came out with their bags, all three trying to shelter under the umbrella as they all walked up to the house and onto the verandah. There Mr. Parry introduced them.

"Colonel, these are some visitors from Kingston trying to find out about the Maroons." Each of the three shook the Colonel's hand. "Can you take care of them?"

The Maroon Colonel smiled. "Yes, Welcome. We're used to visitors. Bring you' bags inside."

"You' in safe hands now. The Colonel will take care of you," Mr. Parry started back to his vehicle. "I will come back for you tomorrow, same time. Me gone to check on mi coffee plants. Hope the mountain don't slide down on them again wid all dis rain."

Inside the small house the living room was cosy. There was carved wooden furniture with embroidered cushions, a sofa covered in a lace cover, a center table decorated with a vase of plastic flowers and framed pictures on the walls of Marcus Garvey, a map of Africa and a pencil drawing of a Black mother and child.

"Come in, come in. We have a room you can sleep in. It has a bunk bed for you girls and we can put a cot for the young man. Sit down and tell me about your mission," the Colonel invited. Soon they were sipping steaming enamel mugs of hot coffee and explaining the reasons they had come to Maroon country in search of Elisabeth's ancestor, a slave named Mercy.

"It's not going to be easy to trace that one woman," the Colonel admitted when they had finished. "The records on paper and the records in our memory are not always clear. Our community of Maroons began in about 1723, when the Maroons in the West, in Trelawny, decided to split up so as to organize the slavery resistance movement. One set of Maroons stayed in Trelawny under leadership of the warrior Kodjo, they organized another tribe in Clarendon and then they sent the woman we call Nanny here to the Blue Mountains of Portland where the largest number of free Africans were living."

"We have heard about Nanny," Elisbeth was quick to show she was not just an ignorant tourist, but knew the relevant history.

"That's good," the Colonel was pleased. "From she came here in about 1720, the great Queen Nanny organized this town so well, they named it Nanny Town after her. The land was about 600 acres and she set it up like an African village. She made the people plant food crops, corn and vegetables and she made them plant a large plantain walk

which was the main food for the village. You know plantain?"
he asked Elisabeth.

"No."

"It is big cousin to banana, you can eat it ripe or
green, fry it or boil it, but I love it most roasted in a coal
fire!" The Colonel laughed. Marshall and Marie exchanged
knowing glances.

"So, we survived far up here in the mountains on our
own for many years. When we needed things, we would send
women down to the towns to exchange food for what we
needed. We had friends on the plantations who would steal
weapons and gunpowder for us and sometimes we would
raid plantations and even burn them down and bring the
slaves back to Nanny Town to live with us and increase our
numbers."

"It was a real revolutionary war!" Marshall was
excited.

"It certainly was!" the Colonel was proud. "We
Maroons were the greatest fighters, better than the English.
The location of the town was well selected by Queen Nanny.
It was on a high ridge overlooking Stony River that no
soldiers could approach by surprise. She had lookouts

everywhere who used the Abeng to speak to us and tell us everything they could see. Queen Nanny took good care of us, like a mother. She knew all about the African healing herbs when we were sick or wounded. She was a priestess, so she led the spiritual life and ceremonies that protected us and kept us alive. She was a great woman."

The visitors nodded in agreement.

"The English attacked Nanny Town three times before they finally occupied it and burnt it to the ground in 1733. It was a sad day, a sad, sad day." The Colonel shook his head and grew silent.

"What happened to Queen Nanny?" Elisabeth and Marie both asked in the same breath.

"They didn't capture her when they captured Nanny Town." The Colonel perked up. "Queen Nanny was way ahead of them. Even while she was building Nanny Town, she had some of her people go further up into the hills and build a few hideouts where only she and her people knew about and could go to. They built shelters just like the little houses you see outside and planted food, so that whenever they had to run away, they could have somewhere to live and take care of themselves.

"The last hideaway she lived at with her people was the place we call Katta-Wood, or Scatta-Wood where we would scatter to if we were attacked. After the last attack in 1733, Queen Nanny took the people who survived into the hills at Katta-Wood and continued to live there and rule for many years."

"Did the English find her and kill her eventually?" Marie asked.

"We don't really know what happened to take the life of Queen Nanny," the Colonel admitted. "Some say she committed suicide by jumping off the ridge over Nanny Town. And some say she flew away back to Africa."

"Flew back to Africa!" Marie was smiling. She turned to Elisabeth. "Remember Bradshaw said that the people could fly! I hope that's what she did for real!"

The Colonel smiled too. "You're a real African, my sister. We Maroons say her spirit is still here with us at Nanny Falls. She comes to visit us when we have a water celebration."

"What is that?" Marie asked.

"Where is Nanny Falls?" Elisabeth asked.

"You people come at a good time. We are having a water celebration under the full moon tonight. Whenever we have a rain like this on full moon night, the spirit gods always bless our celebration the best."

"Spirit gods? Full moon celebration? Tell us more," Elisabeth was intrigued.

"Full moon is always a special time of month for us Maroons. Tonight you will join our celebration and learn more. Come, put your things in the room. You will want to change your wet clothes and take a rest before tonight. "

The Colonel opened the door to a bedroom containing a double bunk bed with a sisal mat on the floor and a small table on which stood a kerosene lamp. He brought a folded cot into the room, which Marshall helped him unfold and then a young girl brought in some sheets and blankets. The lack of sleep the night before, the tension of the morning flight across the island and the drive to Maroon country took their toll on the three, and soon each was fast asleep, lulled by the rhythm of the rain on the zinc roof above them and on the plants and ground outside.

CHAPTER TWENTYFOUR

THE RIVER

"Come. We ready to move now," Colonel Wood said when he woke them in the late evening. "Put on you' walking shoes. The rain kinda ease up, but the ground is slippery. We have a little distance to go."

Colonel himself wore a pair of galoshes, but in place of the neat white shirt, he wore a uniform of sorts consisting of bright red trousers, a red jacket and he was carrying a large wrapped package under his arm. He was not alone.

A line of women and men followed him, dressed in clothes that were clearly kept for special occasions. The women were mostly dressed in white, with bright head wraps in red, blue and gold. As they walked, they repeated a chorus. One woman shook a tambourine, another man tapped a small drum under his arm.

As they walked, others joined along the road heading downhill, about twenty or thirty people singing and keeping beat for the walkers steps with drums, tambourines and sticks beating on metal cans. Marie, Elisabeth and Marshall followed behind the Colonel, walking towards and then in line with the river flowing through the valley.

Soon they came to a clearing beside the river, a flat place next to a beautiful waterfall that flowed only about three feet into a small pool beneath that was crystal blue in colour, shimmering with the continuous splash of water. The Colonel continued walking straight to the water, bent at the riverbank and splashed water on his face, indicating that the visitors should do the same. Each did. The water was icy cold.

"Welcome to Nanny Falls," said Colonel Wood. 'Join us." He turned from the river and pointed to the clearing. In the center was an amazing sight.

Under a canopy of tree branches, a large round table had been set in the center of the clearing. Wide strips of African-patterned fabric had been set radiating out from the center, making a multi-coloured circle. On a pedestal in the center of the circle was an enormous glass bowl filled with water. Circulating around it was a circle of very large wine glasses, then around that a circle of smaller wine glasses, then a circle of glass bowls and finally a circle of crystal drinking glasses. Around the outer edge of the table, on each strip of fabric, were small wine glasses. Some glasses were rimmed with gold, others were engraved with monograms.

All were filled with water.

Interspersed between the many glasses were tall white candles, their light glistening and reflecting in the many glasses of water.

The people who awaited the Colonel were as well-dressed as he. The women wore long, wide satin skirts and long-sleeved satin shirts all embellished with brightly coloured belts and headwraps. Some women who looked especially queenly with gold cloth wrapped in their head-ties and clothing, stood surrounded by a group of what seemed like their courtiers. The men wore long shirts outside trousers and tied their waists with colourful belts, but some stood out with heads covered in similar bright wraps. They were a colourful group.

Some looked over at the visitors and it was obvious they were asking who they were and why they were there.

The three could see the Colonel explaining to one group and smiling in their direction.

"What's going to happen? What is the celebration for?" Elisabeth needed to know.

"I hope it's not what I think it is!" Marie bent to whisper in Elisabeth's ear. "My mother would not like to know where I am right now."

"Why? What's the matter?" Elisabeth was a little worried.

"Never mind. It's a kind of religious celebration we brought from Africa. It's not an approved religion, people like my mother call it 'science'. But don't worry. Just hold on to me and stay by my side, no matter what." Marie took hold of Elisabeth's hand. "Don't let go. Marshall," she turned to her brother, "same thing for you. Stay beside us at all times."

The Colonel uncovered the wrapped object he had carried from the house. It was a gold cardboard crown decorated with plastic jewels, with a flap of cloth edged in gold trim that fell on his shoulders. He placed the crown on his head and it was a signal for the proceedings to begin.

The drummer who had accompanied them to the river was now joined by three more among the crowd of people who had been waiting for everyone's arrival. The company of drummers began a new beat that was faster than the walking beat and the entire body of people started a counter-clockwise dancing march around the table.

The singing increased with more and stronger voices.

The drumming continued stronger, faster. The drum beat, the heartbeat.

The marchers continued their circling of the table, stepping in time to the drum beat, clapping their hands, shaking tambourines, singing.

At first Marie, Elisabeth and Marshall had merely stood at one side, watching the spectacle and waiting for whatever was to happen.

They saw the full moon rise up over the hill that faced the waterfall, whose splashes were now made silver in its light. It seemed bigger and brighter than they had ever seen a full moon.

The marching and singing continued. The marchers did not seem tired.

The heartbeat drumming continued. The drummers did not seem tired.

The drumbeat was the heartbeat. The heart always beats.

Feet were tapped.

Shoulders were moved.

Hands joined in the clapping.

The Colonel came over to the three and led them to the marchers, who eased up enough space for them to join without losing a step.

The marching and singing and drumming continued.

There was a cry, a shriek, a wail of a banshee, as a woman flung herself to the ground, writhing in some kind of fit or madness. Two women stepped out of the line of marchers and picked her up, held down her frantic gestures, moved her to the side of the clearing where other men and women helped hold her, fan her, quiet her down. The other marchers hardly paid any attention to the woman and her strange actions, but Marie and Elisabeth exchanged open-eyed glances, holding each other even more tightly.

And then all of a sudden, Marie and Elisabeth saw a silver stool rise out of the crystal blue pool in the center of the waterfall. A woman sat on the stool dressed in a flowing white gown. Her colour was as black as the riverstones and her features were fully African. A long white scarf flowed from her head to the ground and disappeared into the water of the falls.

The woman stretched her arms wide and reached to Marie and Elisabeth.

CHAPTER TWENTYFIVE

NANNA

Elisabeth and Marie were stunned by what they now saw. They were in a fruitful valley high up in the mountains. From their position they could see for miles and miles in every direction. The Blue Mountains rippled before them on all sides, the tree tops seeming like a rumpled carpet of green shining in the morning sunshine.

Below them they could see the slopes had been planted with rows of vegetable in beds lined up on hillside terraces. On the left the hillside was completely covered in tall plantain trees, heavy with fruit. Men with machetes and women with hoes tilled the gardens. They could hear the laughter of children playing and the music of a lone flute added to the birdsongs all around them.

A beautiful woman stood before them, dressed in a long white gown. Her head was wrapped in white with silver ribbons threaded into the cloth. In her right hand she held a shining machete, with her left hand she beckoned to the girls.

"My daughters! Come to your mother!"

The girls could hear her speak in a voice that was like the rippling sound of the waterfall.

"They took you away, but you have come back. Come to your mother!"

The sight the girls were seeing changed.

Now they saw a vicious battle between Africans and English soldiers in the middle of a Maroon village.

They saw English soldiers burning Maroon houses, Maroons running to escape them.

They saw English soldiers capturing African men, women and children.

The vision clouded and then cleared again. They saw the woman sitting on her silver throne in a large safu yard, surrounded by Maroon warriors.

They heard her speak to a man who stood in front of her:

Kodjo, you fly here to tell me you will sign a Peace with the planters. I have fought the slave-masters three times and defeated them. I will defeat them again. All I need is your help to conquer them, to kill them all and make this land our new Africa. I need you to send your soldiers from Trelawny and from Clarendon to help us fight them here in the East.

The girls saw her wait and listen to the man's reply, then speak again.

We must not give up the fight. This country can be ours. We outnumber them and we are better warriors. That is why they want us to sign for Peace.

They saw her listen to the man standing in front of her.

Your plan to make Peace with our enemy is not a good plan. They are not to be trusted. They will trick you. They will NEVER allow us to be free.

The woman listened again, then her mouth curled in a scornful look.

You are lazy. How can you be satisfied with the small piece of land they say they will give you, when you could have the whole country, from the west to the east.

You are a coward. You are tired of fighting, when you were raised to be a fighter. Our father would be sick to hear you. I am glad he is not here to hear you!

Go on! Fly back to the cockpits. Our warriors will never give up. We will never sign your Treaty! We will fight until this land is OURS!

The vision changed. The girls could see two girl children living on a slave plantation.

They saw the girls growing from babies to girls to young women.

They saw a white planter have brutal sex with one of them.

They saw her sister watch that act, and cry.

They saw the first girl give birth to a brown-skinned child.

They saw that child grow up to young womanhood.

They saw the same White man have sex with her.

They saw that girl give birth to a white-skinned baby.

The woman in the vision rose up and shook her hands in anger.

I SAW YOU TAKE MY DAUGHTER!

I SAW YOU TAKE MY DAUGHTER'S TREASURE!

The woman held her head and wailed.

My children! My beloved daughters.

We had a beautiful village!

We had fields of plantains!

I planted pumpkins!

The woman stepped off her silver throne.

She stretched out her arms wide.

The sleeves of her gown draped over her wrists.

Her dress flowed over her body, young and firm, a muscled stomach, strong thighs.

PIBBA! you went so far away!

AMINA! You stayed here with me!

My daughters have come back to me!

Now we can live together like we used to!

Come let us greet your father Johnny!

Let us fly away home together!

The woman reached out and held each girl by the wrist.

The touch of the woman was soothing, welcoming, cool like the waterfall.

It seemed so right to want to lie down in the woman's arms, to rest in the cool of the river.

As she lay down in the cool of the woman's embrace, Marie heard herself asking:

"What is the message?"

"What is the message!"

"Tell me! We want to know!"

The woman looked at one girl, then at the other and smiled..

Then she spoke in a voice that thundered like the river rolling with large stones.

GIVE ME MY CROWN!

IT IS TIME!

GIVE ME MY CROWN!

The woman reached out and embraced the two girls who were still holding tightly to each other, enfolding them and crushing them to her bosom in a loving embrace.

COME SIT BESIDE ME MY DAUGHTERS.

IT'S COOL HERE.

COME SIT IN YOUR MAMA'S ARMS

CHAPTER TWENTY TWO

THE MESSAGE

Why am I so wet? Marie wondered as she rose up. Why am I on the ground?

Looking around she saw that Elisabeth was also lying beside her. Was she resting, sleeping? Had she been sleeping? Where am I?

"Oh my God! You finally wake up!" It was Marshall shouting, worried and excited. "My God, I think you dead!!! You alright?" There were tears on his face.

"What happened?" Marie was groggy. "Why am I wet?"

"*You nearly drown*!!!" Marshall shouted. "You and Elisabeth decide to take a swim in the river in the middle of the night and the two of you nearly *drown*!!! What happen ... you gone crazy or something? You were screaming and howling and going on bad! I couldn't believe it!" Her brother was both angry and worried.

"I don't believe you!" Marie was shocked. "I was standing beside you all night! I never went for no river swim!"

"I'm telling you! The two of you jumped into the river!" Marshall was upset. "Good thing it was moonlight so we could see you! It took four men to drag you both out! I thought you were both going to drown!" Tears started rolling down Marshall's face.

"Colonel Wood!" he called. "Them wake up! Come!"

Hearing his voice, Elisabeth also stirred, opening her eyes to the same surprise at her surroundings and condition as Marie. Also hearing his voice, Colonel Wood and two women wearing gold crowns on their heads entered the small thatched shelter under the trees where the girls had been laid to recover.

"I'm so glad you girls are alright. You gave us such a fright?" he looked worried.

"What happened?" Marie asked. The Colonel looked at each of them separately then spoke.

"The spirit gods of the water chose you to be their messenger. What did they say?"

"The spirit gods of the water? You've got to be joking!" Elisabeth shook her head.

"Yes," the Colonel's face showed he was serious. "That is who my people came here to speak to and hear from the spirit gods. There are secrets that they only share at full moon time. We need to know what the spirit gods said to you. What was the message?"

"Speak to spirits?" Elisabeth and Marie looked at each in amazement, and then their memory revived to confirm what they had experienced. Marie spoke.

"It was only one spirit. I don't know how I knew to ask her what the message was, but I asked her. She said:

'Give me my crown. It is time. Give me my crown!' "

"Say that again!" the Colonel smiled. "Sounds like we had a visit from Queen Nanny!"

"It was definitely Queen Nanny," Elisabeth spoke firmly. "She said that we were her children who had been taken away from her in the last Maroon war. She showed us

Mercy, from she was a baby! She made us see all the ancestors that were born from her!"

The Colonel clapped his hands and laughed.

"Yes it was Queen Nanny and you brought a good message from the Queen. It is definitely time to give Queen Nanny her crown." The Colonel spoke firmly.

"The government wants to declare Nanny a National Hero. She would be the only woman. Some Maroons say Kodjo should be the Maroon National Hero because he signed the Treaty, but we the Eastern Maroons say Nanny was the real Hero. She didn't sell out and sign over our lives to the British. Nanny said we should fight on until we drive the British out of Jamaica. It took us until we got Independence in 1964 to do that! We would have had it sooner if we had followed Nanny's advice. Yes, it's time to give Queen Nanny her crown!"

"We heard her tell Kodjo not to sign the Treaty." Elisabeth nodded. "She told him they should not stop fighting until the land belonged to all the Black people."

"And we found out who we are!" Marie was laughing. "This White girl and me are descended from two of Nanny's children! We are cousins! She showed us all that!"

Elisabeth nodded her head. "But how was that Nanny? Was it she who made us go into the river? How did that happen? How did the vision come about? How did we see and hear all that? No one would ever believe me if I told them the spirit world is real!"

The Colonel put a finger to his lips. "Shhh. You will not speak of this experience to anyone. One day when you are old, you may tell your children, but they will not believe you. For now, this never happened."

He rose up and from a pocket took a small bottle of oil. Tipping it to his fingers, he anointed the forehead of each girl with the sign of the Cross, then said some words they did not understand, put his hand on his heart and tapped each on the head with the rod of authority he carried.

"We have made stretchers. Four of the men will carry you both back up to the School House. Our celebration will go on till morning. Thank you for being our messengers."

CHAPTER TWENTY TWO

HOMECOMING

"THE AFRICAN PLEDGE

We will Remember the Humanity, Glory and

Sufferings of Our Ancestors.

And Honour THE STRUGGLE OF OUR ELDERS.

We will Strive to Bring NEW VALUES, and

NEWLIFE To Our People.

We will have Peace and Harmony Among US

We will be Loving, Sharing and Creative

We will WORK, STUDY and LISTEN So we may

LEARN, LEARN, so we May Teach

WE WILL CULTIVATE SELF-RELIANCE

WE WILL STRUGGLE TO RESURRECT

AND UNIFY OUR HOMELAND.

WE WILL RAISE MANY CHILDREN

For Our NATION

We will have DISCIPLINE, PATIENCE and COURAGE

We will live as Models to Provide New

DIRECTION For Our People.

We will be FREE and SELF-DETERMINED

WE ARE AFRICAN PEOPLE

WE WILL WIN!!!"

Marie read out loud the sign posted beside the blackboard on the wall of the School House verandah. She had not seen it the day before when they arrived in the rain.

It was raining again, as she, Elisabeth and Marshall descended the steps to Mr. Parry's Land Rover, covered with even more mud than the day before. The Colonel covered them with his huge umbrella as they said goodbye, giving each a strong handshake and a white cotton napkin tied around hot, crispy fried plantain slices.

"Come and visit us again. It was good to have you here," he said with a smile.

A woman sat in the back seat of Mr. Parry's vehicle. "Introduce yourselves, ladies." He gestured to the two girls as he drove off down the waterlogged road back to the town. "This lady is Mrs. Richards ... she teaches my son's class at Tichtfield School in Port Antonio ... I'm giving her a lift down to the town."

The woman smiled, bowed politely and shook fingers with each girl.

"I am Marie Grant, this is my brother Marshall, and this is my cousin from England, Elisabeth Grant," Marie explained.

"Grant? Related to the Grant Scholarship Grants?" she inquired.

"Grant Scholarship?" The girls were open-mouthed.

"Yes. The Grant Scholarship for one Maroon girl each year since the school was founded in 1786. Don't know why it's called the Grant scholarship, because it's given by a family named Falmouth. A lady named Mercy Falmouth started it ... can never forget her name ... Mercy."

"I can't believe it!!" Elisabeth was shouting, slapping Marie on the shoulder as they both rejoiced at this surprising information. "This is just a miracle! Yes, it's my family! Grant is my family name. The first Lord Falmouth was Captain James Grant. And Grant was Marie's mother's name, after the slavemaster who owned her."

Elisabeth was rocking up and down on the back seat in happy excitement, Marie was laughing at her, while Marshall smiled from his seat in front. Mrs. Richards was shocked at the effect her words had on her travel companions.

Marie explained. "We have been looking for a lost member of the Grant family. We thought we would never find her, but you just found the needle in the haystack. Are you sure about this Grant scholarship?"

"Yes," Mrs. Edwards was certain, a bit peeved at being doubted. "We teachers know the history of our school. Every year a bank in England sends money from the Falmouth account to fund the scholarship. It's not awarded every year, because it's not every year that there is a Maroon girl to receive it. But it's there on the books. I can take you and show you, if you wish."

"I'd definitely like to do that, please." said Elisabeth. "Mr. Parry, can you recommend a good hotel in Port Antonio where we can get a hot bath, a clean bed and a good meal? I'd like to stay in this part of Jamaica for another day or two."

"I'll take you up to the DeMontevin Lodge on Titchfield Hill. It's right next to the school and you and Mrs. Edwards can arrange to meet."

"I hope it has a phone," Marshall was concerned. "I have to call our mother and tell her we're OK and then I have to find the band."

* * * *

The De Montevin Lodge had a phone, with an extension in each room. Elisabeth paid for three rooms.

The first phone call eased their mother's worry. "Everything's OK, as long as you children are alright, Marie. Come home soon."

The second phone call was to the band's Kingston headquarters. "The bus is fixed and they're heading back to reach Kingston tomorrow," Marshall reported. Marie smiled. She would soon see Tony again. She was looking forward to continuing their conversation.

The third phone call was from Elisabeth to Mark in England.

"No, I'm fine ... Yes, I found what I was looking for ...

"Guess what! I'm Black! Yes!... And guess what! I love being Black! ... No, I'm not going crazy ...

"No, I'm not coming back right away ... going to spend some time in Jamaica ... it's lovely here ...might buy some land ...

"Give my love to your Mother ... Bye..."

The fourth phone call was also from Elisabeth, this one to Bradshaw asking if he had some way to come and get them.

He arrived the next day driving an older model BMW.

"So glad to see you. Love the car," Elisabeth teased.

"How did you think I was coming ... by plane again?"

"I was wondering," she laughed.

"Ever thought about an upgrade to that toy plane?"

"Frankly, Blondie," Bradshaw was serious for a moment. "My dream is to have a fleet of small planes flying tourists instead of fertilizer. All it takes is money!"

It was Elisbeth's turn to smile.

"I have lots of that."

Printed in Great Britain
by Amazon

17375782R00210